"Dr. Angela Neal-Barnett's wisdom, direction, and practical techniques for addressing and managing anxiety, panic, and fear are right on time for a nation of Black women who are sick and tired of being sick, tired, and afraid. *Soothe Your Nerves* will be a must-have on my clients' resource reading guide. Dr. Neal-Barnett helps to shatter the old myths of what it means to be a strong Black woman while giving us encouraging wisdom on being today's healthy Black woman. Thanks so much for your wisdom."—Julia A. Boyd, psychotherapist and author of *Can I Get a Witness?*

"Dr. Angela Neal-Barnett uncovers a much ignored problem and identifies strategies for healing the effects of anxiety on women's lives. This is a book for everyone. There are few psychologists who can tell the stories of those who have suffered from anxiety disorders. Dr. Neal-Barnett speaks for others as no one else can. Let the healing begin."—Gail Elizabeth Wyatt, Ph.D., author of *Stolen Women: Reclaiming Our Sexuality, Taking Back Our Lives* and coauthor of *No More Clueless Sex: Ten Sexual Secrets that Can Work for Both of You*

"*Soothe Your Nerves* addresses the major 'invisible' health issues for women of color: anxiety, panic, and fear! Dr. Barnett provides a comprehensive explanation, in laymen's terms, of the causes and predisposing factors of these emotional conditions and their destructive effects on Black women. She offers self-help exercises and commonsense, workable solutions that range from conventional medicine to holistic and spiritual treatments. A must-read for women, men, and treatment professionals, *Soothe Your Nerves* offers hope and healing, which will invariably result in the empowerment of Black women in all aspects of their lives."—Dr. Jeff Gardere, television and radio host, author of *Love Prescription*

"The sin and shame is not in suffering from an anxiety disorder. The sin and shame is in failing to call it what it is and in not getting the help we need and deserve as African-American women. Dr. Angela Neal-Barnett helps us face our disorders and shows us where to turn for help."—Renita J. Weems, Ph.D., author of *Showing Mary* and *Just a Sister Away*

"*Soothe Your Nerves* by Dr. Angela Neal-Barnett is a *must-read* for all women of color. The information is extremely valuable and presented in a manner that allows Dr. Neal-Barnett's message to hit home. Even if you don't suffer from 'nerves,' you need to read this book and become better informed about the conditions that may affect the well-being of the women in your life."—Anita Bunkley, author of *Mirrored Life*

"As a Community Activist, primarily in the African-American community, I witness many women who unfortunately carry the weight of the world on their shoulders. In *Soothe Your Nerves*, Dr. Angela Neal-Barnett has provided us with the key that will unlock the shackles of pressure. By defining our anxieties, we can realize that we no longer have to buy the bacon and fry it up in a pan. We are free at last!"—Yvonne Pointer-Triplet, author of *Behind the Death of a Child*

SOOTHE YOUR NERVES

The Black Woman's Guide to Understanding and Overcoming Anxiety, Panic, and Fear

DR. ANGELA NEAL-BARNETT

A Fireside Book

Published by Simon & Schuster

New York · London · Toronto · Sydney · Singapore

FIRESIDE
Rockefeller Center
1230 Avenue of the Americas
New York, NY 10020

FIRESIDE and colophon are registered trademarks of Simon & Schuster, Inc.

For information about special discounts for bulk purchases,
please contact Simon & Schuster Special Sales:
1-800-456-6798 or business@simonandschuster.com

Designed by Lisa Stokes

Manufactured in the United States of America

1   3   5   7   9   10   8   6   4   2

Library of Congress Cataloging-in-Publication Data
Neal-Barnett, Angela M., 1960–
Soothe your nerves: the Black woman's guide to understanding and overcoming
    anxiety, panic, and fear / Angela Neal-Barnett.
p. cm.
Includes index.
1. African American women—Mental health. 2. Panic disorders. 3. Fear.
    4. Anxiety. I. Title.
RC451.5.N4N43 2003
362.2'089'96073—dc21   2003045634

ISBN 0-7432-2538-4

For the anxious Black women I knew as a child and didn't have the knowledge and skills to help, for anxious Black women everywhere who want to reclaim their lives, and for Pop-Pop up in heaven

CONTENTS

*L*ATELY, EVERY TIME I go to church, I miss church. I'm *in* the building; I just rarely make it to the sanctuary. When I do, the choir has sung and the sermon's half over. Every Sunday for the past year I've left the house with my husband and preschooler determined to participate in an entire service. It hasn't happened. Instead, somewhere between children's church and the sanctuary, I am stopped by somebody who really *needs to talk.*

And it's not just at church. These days it seems everywhere I go, someone wants to speak with me. At the grocery store, at funerals, at the library, even at the carousel in the mall, someone is always stopping me. When I go into my office, it's the same thing. My e-mail and voice mail are filled with messages from women who *need to talk.*

What do these women want to talk to me about? What is so important that they lay in wait for me on a Sunday morning, seek me out in public places, and e-mail me halfway across the country? Anxiety and fear, only that's not what they call it.

"Nerves," they say, or "This situation is working my last nerve" or "My nerves are bad." Because I am a psychologist who specializes in anxiety among African-American women, they believe talking or writing to me will make it better. What they fail to realize, and what I gently point out, is that talking to me in the hallway for a few minutes during church, snatching a few minutes with me in the cereal aisle, or receiving an e-mail reply from me is not sufficient. Overcoming anxiety and fear involves a daily plan of action.

As these women share their stories, I am reminded of the first Black woman I ever met with bad nerves. Her name was Mrs. Golden Williams, and she was the lead soprano in the Prince of Peace AME Church choir. When I was a teenager, Prince of Peace was famous for its choir. Many of the members had sung professionally, and the choir director had sung with the Fisk Jubilee Singers. People actually came to church on time so that they wouldn't miss the choir. There were a number of great singers in that choir, but Mrs. Williams was the best. She had a five-octave range and sounded to me a lot like Minnie Riperton. Her signature song was "It Is Well with My Soul." I used to get goose bumps every time she sang the last line. One Sunday, Mrs. Williams wasn't in the choir. She missed the next three Sundays, showed up, sang "It Is Well with My Soul," and, to my knowledge, never came to church or sang in the choir again.

Twelve Sundays later, after sitting through Mrs. Bancroft's pale rendition of the song, I asked my friend Jackie, who at fifteen knew all the church's business, what happened to Mrs. Williams. "Angie," Jackie said, "Mrs. Williams has bad nerves."

Not long after Jackie told me this, I witnessed Mrs. Williams's bad nerves for myself. I was in the grocery store with my father when I noticed a familiar figure in the produce section. It was

Mrs. Williams, but she looked odd. She was breathing funny and clutching her chest. She ran up to my father and begged him to help her. He walked her to the front of the store and arranged for one of the bag boys to drive her home. When he returned, he shook his head and said, "It's her nerves."

It wasn't until years later, when I was training to be a psychologist, that I realized Mrs. Williams's bad nerves had another name: anxiety. Knowing what I know now about anxiety, I believe Mrs. Williams became so afraid of getting nervous that she stopped going places. She stopped singing, and the congregation lost a voice that had been soothing to their souls. She stopped shopping and had meals delivered to her home. Eventually, she stopped going anywhere and just stayed home. Until the day she died, Mrs. Williams never went farther than her own backyard.

Over the course of fifteen years of research on anxiety among African Americans, I've met, talked, counseled, and listened to hundreds of Mrs. Williamses—beautiful, talented Black women with bad nerves. There was Maya, a lawyer whose fear of criticism and failure kept her from being promoted; Willa Mae, a lifelong friend of my mother's whose fear of cats caused her to stand in the middle of our driveway and holler whenever she came to visit; and Tee, who appeared to have it all but whose anxiety made it impossible for her to go anywhere but to work and back. In this book I'll share their stories and the stories of others whose debilitating anxiety and fear prevented them from being all the Creator intended them to be. Each of the women you will meet in this book thought that Black women didn't get anxious. Each of them felt as if they had lost control of their lives. Many of them had. The good news is most were able to regain control.

Through the years as I've talked with anxious Black women, regardless of their age, income, or status in life, the first question they always ask me is "Why?" "Why is this happening to me?" "Why am I afraid?" "Why can't I get over this?" Black women can spend years trying to find out why they are anxious and fearful, and if and when they do, it doesn't make a difference. The anxiety and fear still remain. In fact, the search for why can increase the anxiety and fear. The key to overcoming anxiety and fear is not *why* but *what*. What is anxiety? What is fear? What effect are they having on my life? What can I do to overcome them?

WHAT IS ANXIETY?

Anxiety is the perception or awareness of a future threat. An anxious Black woman "just knows" something bad is going to happen. She doesn't know what, she doesn't know when, but in her mind she truly believes terrible things will come to pass. This imagined bad thing is called a perceived future threat. This type of threat is unrealistic and far worse than anything that actually happens. However, to a Black woman who is experiencing anxiety, it feels very real. The fact that it feels so real creates a sense of apprehension or impending doom. The mere thought of the perceived threat places a Black woman in a state of being constantly on guard and agitated, known as hypervigilance. She is always watching and waiting for the threat to occur. Her senses are sharpened, her muscles are tight, and she is perpetually waiting for the other shoe to drop. Hypervigilance can be exhausting and create impairment or cautiousness in one's performance. As a result, many anxious Black women choose either to play it safe or not to play at all.

Sheila was the DJ for a popular morning radio show. Listeners were drawn to her bright and bubbly manner. Recently named the most popular media personality in the state, Sheila was very proud of her work and her accomplishments. The station owners were so pleased with her success they gave her a huge raise and a car. But lately Sheila felt uncomfortable when she was on the air. She couldn't quite put her finger on what was wrong; all she knew was she couldn't shake the feeling that disaster was around the corner. As these feelings increased, she felt more and more on edge, and it became harder and harder for her to complete her shift. Realizing she couldn't continue this way, last week Sheila announced she was giving up her radio show indefinitely.

WHAT IS FEAR?

Fear is a related emotion but somewhat different from anxiety. Whereas anxiety is the result of an imagined or perceived threat, fear is brought on by an imminent or immediate threat. A fearful Black woman has a physical reaction to the threat. Her heart may start to beat faster, her breathing may become shallower, and she may start to shake. When a Black woman is experiencing fear, she makes one of two choices: flight or fright. The woman who chooses flight runs away or avoids the thing or situation that makes her afraid. The woman who chooses fright remains in the situation or presence of the thing or person that makes her fearful, but the fear paralyzes her and renders her powerless.

I can see some of you shaking your heads as you read this section. Common sense says that when you are in danger, of course you run! But there is a difference between the commonsense healthy form of fear and debilitating fear. The fear we experience while crossing the street and a car is bearing down on us that we didn't see until the last minute helps us jump out of the way more quickly. The fear we experience when we are caught in the middle of a thunderstorm reminds us to seek shelter quickly. But fear that is chronic and prevents us from doing things that we want is not healthy and is detrimental to our well-being.

For as long as I can remember, Billie wanted to be a doctor. When we were seniors in high school, she won a full scholarship to a combined college/medical school program, a full scholarship to Cornell, and a full scholarship to the local university. She turned them all down and went into a two-year nursing program. When I asked her why, she said, "I'm scared I'll fail. When they offered me those scholarships, my whole body started shaking, and I just wanted to run away screaming no. I just can't do it, Angie. I'm just too scared."

I was stunned. Billie had never received a grade lower than an A in her life. Calculus and physics were a breeze to her. She had wanted to be a doctor longer than I had wanted to be a psychologist, and I had wanted to be a psychologist since I was twelve. I couldn't understand her action. I now know the emotional and physical aspects of her fear made her too afraid to try.

FIVE FORMS OF ANXIETY AND FEAR

In *Soothe Your Nerves*, you will learn about five common forms of anxiety and fear:

1. *Panic attacks.* Panic attacks are the most well known form of anxiety. Many Black women mistakenly refer to panic attacks as anxiety attacks. A panic attack consists of a short, clear-cut period of apprehension and fear that

is accompanied by physical symptoms such as sweating, rapid heart rate, and difficulty breathing.

2. *Social phobia.* Fear of being criticized in social or performance situations. You may hear some psychologists refer to it as social anxiety disorder.

3. *Specific phobia.* Fear that occurs in the presence of objects, animals, or nonevaluative, nonperformance situations.

4. *Generalized anxiety.* A chronic, debilitating form of anxiety involving excessive worry and physical tension.

5. *Obsessive-compulsive disorder.* Anxiety characterized by intrusive thoughts and the ritualistic behaviors that attempt to control them.

These forms of anxiety cost this country over $63 billion in lost wages, slower work production, medical visits, and nonmedical treatment. The material price tag is overshadowed by the incalculable emotional costs. Anxiety and fear exact a toll on Black women's physical, emotional, and spiritual lives. Unchecked, they can cost us time with our children, more-loving relationships with our spouses and significant others, friendships and personal relationships, and the deferment or death of our dreams.

It doesn't have to be this way. I cannot tell you how many anxious, fearful Black women I have met and continue to meet, who with the proper knowledge and understanding could begin the journey to overcome their anxiety. But information and understanding about anxiety and how it manifests itself is not readily available in many Black communities. As a result, Black women try to deal with anxiety problems the best way they know how. Unfortunately, the methods they use to cope often make the problem worse.

Some Black women choose to engage in self-medication by drinking alcohol or using drugs. They fail to realize that once the effects of the alcohol or drugs wear off, they're just as anxious as before—and on top of that they're hung over. Some Black women choose to rely on their faith, believing that if it was just a little stronger, they would be delivered. When their fear and anxiety don't go away, they blame themselves for a lack of faith. What follows for many is a period of depression that goes along with the anxiety.

Other Black women believe being anxious is their lot in life. They think no one or no thing can help them. These women are caught up in a negative cycle of thoughts brought on by their anxious state. One of the biggest problems with anxiety is that it perpetuates "what if" thinking. Even after the physical experience of anxiety is gone, the "what if" thinking remains: "What if" it happens again? "What if" I mess up? "What if" what you tell me in this book doesn't help? That is why, once the physical symptoms are alleviated, women must work on the mental component, the anxious "what if" thoughts.

As African-American women, we are descendants of queens of the Nile. When it comes to anxiety and fear, many of us are queens of denial. Even though we know something is wrong, we decide that we are not going to admit it to ourselves or anyone else. In a way it makes sense: If we admit to being anxious, we might find ourselves in a worse emotional state than we are already in. Denial, however, can keep anxiety at bay for only a little while.

THAT WAS THEN, THIS IS NOW

Twenty-five years have passed since I witnessed Mrs. Williams's bad nerves in the grocery store. Back then, the information I share in this book wasn't available. Twenty-five years ago Black women weren't anxious; they suffered from what psychologists called excessive nervousness or neurosis. Black folks said it was bad nerves and, like my father, just shook their heads when they talked about these women.

Times have changed. Today we know that bad nerves are another name for anxiety, and anxiety has various forms. Slowly but surely Black women are gaining an awareness of anxiety and its debilitating effects. Over the past two years the Black women's magazines *Essence* and *Heart and Soul* have featured articles on panic attacks, generalized anxiety, and social anxiety. The popular Showtime TV drama *Soul Food* features a main character, Terry, a successful Black woman who has developed panic attacks. The show's realistic portrayal of panic and its associated behaviors put a Black perspective on this particular form of anxiety.

It's twenty-five years too late for Mrs. Golden Williams; she and her wonderful voice departed this life without ever finding a way to soothe her nerves. But it is not too late for other Black women who want to overcome anxiety and fear. This book was written for you. So little is spoken or written about Black women and anxiety that many of you believe you are the only one suffering. Nothing could be further from the truth. Written from a psychological, spiritual, and Black perspective, this book is a guide for understanding and overcoming anxiety disorder. As you read, you may recognize yourself or someone you love. It is my hope you will also recognize that you are not alone and that various forms of help are available. By the time you reach the end of this book, you will have the information necessary for developing a plan to overcome the anxiety and fear in your life.

I | BAD NERVES

ONE

◈

What Caused This to Happen to Me?

CALLIE WAS THE MOTHER of four-year-old twins, the wife of a public official, and a university professor. The demands on her time, the discrimination she experienced on the job, and her role as a public person's spouse combined to make her tense and on edge. She always seemed to be waiting for the other shoe to drop. Callie liked to bake, and baking and eating seemed to calm her nerves. She made big batches of chocolate chip cookies and ate half the dough. Once the cookies were done, she ate half of them. Sometimes for dinner she made wonderful pizzas with four cheeses and an assortment of toppings. Callie would eat three or four slices and then finish up whatever the kids had left on their plates. Before she knew it, she had gained fifty pounds. Part of her knew she had to stop, but eating relieved some of the tension. Could she really give it up?

The answer came fairly quickly. The weight gain began to impact her health. She developed hypertension, and her cholesterol level was sky-high. Her doctor told her that if she wanted to see her twins grow up, she needed to exercise and change her diet. Callie began walking three miles a day. This not only helped her lose weight, but it helped reduce some of the stress she'd been feeling. One day she dropped by my Rise Sally Rise®office and shared about the anticipatory anxiety and panic attacks she was experiencing. I referred her to an anxiety clinic in the area. The lifestyle changes coupled with professional therapy allowed Callie to go from being an anxious, overweight woman to one who was normal weight, confident, and anxiety free.

Glenda, a single mother and postal worker, discovered that alcohol calmed her nerves. Whenever she felt anxious, she took a drink. She often felt anxious when she was out with friends. The drinking reached the point where she would pass out in the street. Her live-in boyfriend became so disgusted that he left. Ultimately, she ended up in a detox center, where she realized her main problem wasn't the alcohol, it was her anxiety.

Clarice, a manager in a hair care company, started having panic attacks at age twenty-nine. One day while sitting in a routine meeting, she began to have trouble breathing and hot flashes. She excused herself, went to the restroom, and splashed water on her face. It didn't help. Somehow she made it through the meeting, but she was anxious and terrified it would happen again. An occasional drug user, she found cocaine made her forget about the anxiety. Soon she went from cocaine to crack. It worked quicker. She lost her job, her luxury car, and her apartment, and eventually moved in with her mother. She knew she needed help, but if she had to choose between the anxiety and the crack, she would choose the crack. One day she woke up and thought, "I just can't do this anymore." Clarice put on her clothes and walked down the street to the bridge overlooking the Cuyahoga River. As she stood there, preparing to jump, she heard a voice telling her she was not alone. She stepped back, then she caught the bus to the Spiritual Way substance abuse support group at her church.

Overeating, drinking, and drug use are the effects of anxiety. The question is how did these women become anxious in the first place? What caused the anxiety that led to their self-destructive behavior?

I wish there was a simple answer to what causes debilitating, life-controlling anxiety, but there isn't. If there was just one reason for women developing severe anxiety, we could eliminate that thing from our lives or, better yet, develop a shot that would make severe anxiety nonexistent. The causes of debilitating anxiety are complex and involve a combination of biological, psychological, and social/environmental factors. Some psychologists combine the words and say that the causes of anxiety are biopsychosocial.

STRESS

Initially, Glenda blamed her anxiety on her man and her kids. If they didn't get on her nerves so bad, she wouldn't have to use alcohol to calm them. Glenda's children and boyfriend did contribute to the development of her anxiety, but not in the way Glenda portrayed it. Glenda was a single Black woman trying to balance a job, a relationship, and children. When the children didn't follow her instructions, as children are likely to do, or interrupted or misbehaved, or when the relationship hit a low point, as is natural in a relationship, or something went wrong at work, the amount of her stress derived from each of these roles increased. Glenda's response to the increased stress produced more stress, which combined with other psychological, environmental, and biological factors to produce crippling anxiety. Common life stressors for women include the birth or death of a child, the loss of a spouse, divorce, marriage, moving, a new job, the loss of a job, the death of a parent or sibling, health issues, and relationships with children.

When I talk with Black women who are mothers, the situations that seem to generate the greatest amount of stress involve their children, particularly incarceration and pregnancy. As mothers, we want better for our children, and dream big dreams for them. When an unplanned pregnancy occurs or a detention center or jail sentence is handed down, many Black mothers I interview initially see it as the end of their dreams. Later they come to understand that their original assumption was not necessarily correct. Once this realization takes hold, they become focused on not allowing the pregnancy or criminal act to ruin their child's life. This positive action can create more stress as they seek out services, help arrange child care, visit on a regular basis, and investigate programs that will help their child achieve against the odds.

PREJUDICE AND DISCRIMINATION AS STRESSORS

Institutional discrimination and interpersonal prejudice are two of the most potent psychological and environmental burdens faced by Black women. Psychologist John Dovidio and his research team define institutional discrimination as an act that takes place when the policies and procedures of an organization or company unfairly restrict the opportunities of African Americans or other minority groups or perpetuate advantages or privileges for the majority group. Interpersonal prejudice is defined as actions and behaviors by colleagues that reflect negative beliefs, attitudes, and feelings toward members of minority groups.

Prejudice and discrimination are insidious stressors that affect Black women of all socioeconomic classes. In the workplace, Black women are often seen as twofers, Black and female; by hiring a Black woman you get two minorities for the price of one. Sometimes this places Black women in double jeopardy, forcing them to deal with prejudice and discrimination targeted at both their race and their sex. Whether we are experiencing prejudice and discrimination because we are Black, because we are female, or because we are both, these behaviors take a toll on us physically and emotionally. One outward emotional expression of that toll is anxiety.

Little attention is paid to the anxiety aspect of prejudice and discrimination. Rather, the spotlight has been on anger, as documented in Ellis Cose's excellent book, *Rage of the Privileged Class*. Anger and anxiety are closely related. Both quicken your heart rate and heighten your level of arousal. When you think about whatever it is that is making you angry or anxious, you become angrier or more anxious. When we as Black women encounter prejudice and discrimination, we are likely to experience both emotions.

In Callie's case, the stress of being a wife, mother, and professor, coupled with the rampant interpersonal prejudice and institutional discrimination in her department, caused her anxiety to move from a manageable to an unmanageable state. Little incidents kept happening; for example, the locks on her office suite were changed, but no one informed her. For the past two semesters the chair's secretary had lost her grades. Arriving early one morning, she overheard three senior professors discussing over coffee what to do about giving that "colored girl" a promotion.

In meetings and university social settings, Callie was often the only person of color and was frequently called upon to give the Black perspective. Her research had won several prestigious awards and earned her national acclaim, but it was on Black women's literature, a topic that her colleagues told her was too narrow and unfocused. Ironically, the chair's new, young second wife's area of expertise was lesbian literature. Although she had neither the national acclaim nor the prestige that Callie did, departmental colleagues heralded her work as "encompassing" and "groundbreaking."

Eventually, the situation reached the point where Callie found herself constantly on guard, hyperalert, and apprehensively waiting for the next—and she knew there would be a next—incident of discrimination or prejudice. She began scrutinizing the remarks of everyone, from senior faculty to students to the custodial staff, for evidence of prejudice. Every action the department took was analyzed for any hint of discrimination. The process was exhausting and made her tense, more worried, more on edge, and mad. As she put it, "No one else has to deal with this mess but me."

As Black women climb the corporate ladder, earn degrees, and change income brackets, the type of prejudice and discrimination encountered becomes more divisive, subtler, and more likely to happen on a daily basis. As a result, she may find herself growing anxious and resentful doing a job that "gets on her nerves" in a field she loves.

Benita's job was working her last nerve. Things had gotten to the point where just thinking about her employment situation caused a panic attack. Benita started out in the city's transportation department cleaning buses. Taking advantage of the tuition reimbursement program, she earned an associate degree in business and worked her way up from the custodial crew to shift supervisor; in this position she dispensed paychecks, assigned buses, developed schedules, and helped prepare a budget. When an assistant manager's position opened up, she applied for it. Everyone just knew she would get the job. She didn't; in fact, she wasn't even interviewed.

"They told me they decided not to interview anyone who already worked here," she said. "They wanted someone from the outside who could bring a fresh perspective. So who did they hire? Some white guy with a high school diploma who was a shift supervisor in the city hall cafeteria! Then they had the gall to ask me to help train him. I don't want to, but I'm afraid if I don't, they won't give me a good recommendation if I try to leave. My stomach always seems to be in knots, and I can't shake the feeling that something else is going to happen."

STRESS, ANXIETY, AND STRONG BLACK WOMEN

Whether it is discrimination, prejudice, or another stressor, Black women appear to handle stress somewhat differently from men or white women. Men are more likely to do battle with whoever or whatever is causing stress, or they simply remove themselves from the situation. White women seem more likely to find stress relief by devoting time to their children or seeking support and friendship from others. Stress researchers call this a "tend and befriend" response. Black women's stress responses are intriguing; we tend, befriend, mend, and keep it in. As Black women we have, as Toni Morrison so eloquently puts it, "invented ourselves." Much of what we have invented to define ourselves as Black women has been resourceful and productive. We are loyal and loving. Many of us know how to persist and persevere. We are creative and have vast experience making a way out of no way. Without a doubt, Black women are the most resilient members of the human race. To paraphrase Maya Angelou, when you try to keep us down, still we rise. This ability to rise against overwhelming odds leads to the concept of the Strong Black Woman.

There are many positives to being a Strong Black Woman. We are ingenious, confident, sassy, and bold. By the same token there are drawbacks, perhaps the biggest being that many women who see themselves as Strong Black Women will keep on keeping on even when they know they should stop. It is as if we feel that to acknowledge we are stressed out or need to rest is akin to giving up membership in the Strong Black Woman club. The opposite of strong is weak, and to pair the words weak and Black woman is to create an oxymoron. In the minds of many Blacks and Whites, a weak Black woman simply does not exist. Rather than being seen as less than she is supposed to be, a Strong Black Woman refuses to admit she is stressed and keeps her feelings and emotions bottled up inside while she helps everyone else. This strategy makes the Strong Black Woman an excellent candidate for the development of anxiety.

Several years ago I conducted a study where self-identified Strong Black Women—women who told us that being strong was an important part of who they were—filled out a diary detailing their activities and emotions. At the same time their blood pressure and heart rate were being monitored. This was done for an entire day. In the diaries the women did not admit to being stressed, even in stressful situations. Marlo wrote, "Had to fire S. today. She didn't take it very well." Firing someone is a stressful situation. Yet the only emotion Marlo indicated that she experienced was calm.

But her blood pressure and heart rate readings told a different story. When firing S., Marlo's blood pressure increased by fifteen points, and a 20-point increase was seen in her heart rate. She wasn't the only one. Almost every woman in the study exhibited the same pattern. Either these women could not admit to being stressed, or they were unaware they were stressed. Interviews indicated that women were aware of their stress level; they were just unwilling to admit it was problematic. Several said to me, "Baby, I don't have time to think about that mess. If I did, I'd be stressed out about everything." Yet taking the time out to acknowledge the stress and do something about it would go a long way toward preventing the development of serious anxiety and the health problems associated with it: chronic upper respiratory infections, hypertension, heart disease, and obesity.

THE FAMILY FACTOR

As Glenda began to confront her past in detox, she realized that her grandmother had also suffered from bad nerves. Glenda's discovery is not unusual. One of the most eye-opening experiences for many Black women comes when they share their anxiety difficulties with a close family member. The family member usually reveals that others in the family are struggling or have struggled with the same problem. In fact, Black women who have a relative with an anxiety problem are seven to nine times more likely to also have that anxiety problem. For many African-American families, anxiety problems are a long-held family secret.

The familial component of anxiety may be biological, environmental, or both. Several years ago Canadian researchers discovered a genetic link for panic attacks. They discovered that people suffering from panic attacks had a gene that increased levels of a chemical called cholecystokinin, or CCK, in their brain. This is not to say that panic attacks are genetically inherited, but people born with this gene are more susceptible to developing panic attacks.

A family history of anxiety difficulties may not necessarily indicate a biological cause for your anxiety. It may instead indicate that your anxiety has environmental roots. If an anxious parent, grandparent, or other family member raised you, your anxiety may have developed partly by simply listening and observing. Our parental figures are our first teachers, our first role models. Our earliest speech and behavior are learned from them. If our parents always wring their hands and talk aloud about their nerves being bad or of being scared, as children we are likely to pick up on it and begin to copy their behavior. If we observe our mothers and grandmothers avoiding situations or people who make them nervous, we learn to do the same thing.

Glenda realized that as a child she had never learned how to deal with situations that made her nervous. Her grandmother tended to avoid or withdraw from anxiety-producing situations. So did her mother. As a teenager and as a young adult Glenda modeled her mother's and grandmother's behavior; she avoided situations. As she grew older, Glenda found that with alcohol she could tolerate some anxiety-provoking situations. In reality, Glenda's alcoholism was another form of avoidance. When she drank, she didn't have to deal with what was really bothering her. Glenda had never been exposed to healthy ways of coping with anxiety. Avoidance was all she knew. Glenda realized that if she was going to overcome her anxiety, she would have to learn other ways of dealing with anxiety-producing situations.

HORMONE IMBALANCE

Over the past decade much has been made of the role chemical imbalances play in the manifestation of emotional difficulties. Certain hormonal imbalances can place women at higher risk for developing anxiety problems. Lower levels of the "female" hormones estrogen and progesterone are associated with an increase in panic attacks. When women who experience panic attacks become pregnant or breast-feed, the levels of these hormones increase, and the number of panic attacks decreases.

Menopause becomes a time of high risk for the development of various forms of anxiety. Women experience a decrease in their estrogen levels during menopause, and for some manageable anxiety increases and becomes unmanageable. In her enlightening pamphlet, *Menopause—the Mean-Pause?* (1997), Clissie Rogers gives a firsthand account of the anxiety difficulties that can arise when a Black woman enters this phase of life. In the poem that opens the compilation, Mrs. Rogers describes her bouts with anxiety and fear:

Help!
Is there any help out there for me?
What is happening to me?
These night sweats
These singeing hot flashes!
I don't want to go anywhere, do anything.
My mind is racing! It sometimes feels that it is going to leave
  me.
I'm angry. I'm yelling.
I'm glad I can sleep so I welcome it.
Why am I having these mood swings, these crazy feelings?

Do I need to be committed?
I used to be so active, so in control, but I'm going to pieces.
Help!

Although several of the women in her church and her male pastor suggested she was going through the change of life, she did not believe them. Only after checking herself into the stress management unit of the local hospital and receiving antianxiety medication and counseling did she begin to consider what others were saying. Mrs. Rogers found that once she began to take her synthetic estrogen, progesterone, and a natural herbal remedy, her hormonal levels increased and the anxiety symptoms significantly decreased.

Another hormone that plays a role in anxiety development is serotonin. You may be less familiar with this hormone; it is also considered a neurotransmitter and is not associated with female reproduction. All the same, low serotonin levels are associated with an increased risk for developing anxiety.

TRAUMA AND LOSS

Trauma and loss are important psychological contributors to the development of anxiety in Black women. African Americans are three to five times more likely to experience trauma through violence and victimization than Whites. Women are more likely to develop a form of debilitating anxiety from a traumatic event than men. They are also likely to suffer from the debilitating anxiety for a longer period of time than men. A high proportion of Black women who suffer from debilitating anxiety are victims of sexual trauma.

Sexual Assault

Several years ago I conducted a study of anxious middle-class Black women, funded by the National Institute of Mental Health (NIMH). Twenty percent of these women were the victims of sexual trauma. In most cases a spouse or significant other, someone they thought they loved and could trust, had sexually violated them. Many kept the incident to themselves until they were interviewed for this study, and then the stories came tumbling out. For a number of the women, sharing the stories of trauma and violence was cathartic. Yet the effects of the trauma colored their entire view of life. They were constantly on edge, always waiting for something bad to happen, always in a state of high anxiety.

It was during this study that Clarice, the hair care company manager mentioned earlier in this chapter, shared her story. As a college student Clarice attended a fraternity party with a close male friend; during the evening he drugged her drink. When she came to, she was lying on the floor; her pants were down to her ankles, and the close male friend was climbing off her as another young man was preparing to climb on top of her. At that moment Clarice's roommate burst into the room and screamed. The young men fled. Clarice and her roommate made a pact never to tell anyone what had happened that night. They never did, and Clarice buried the incident in the deepest part of her memory. With support from her Spiritual Way group and me, Clarice sought therapy for the hidden trauma. Today, Clarice is panic free and helping others to overcome anxiety.

Witnessing Violence

Over time, the repeated witnessing of violence may have the same effect as being a victim of violence. Women who are witnesses to violence are known as co-victims. Co-victimization appears highest among Black women. Watching friends and loved ones be gunned down, beat down, or slapped around takes a toll on our emotions and spirit. As one woman in my NIMH study shared, "I've lost a brother, an uncle, and a cousin to violence. I can't help but wonder will I be next?" This wondering often turns into worry and the tendency to be supervigilant about harm befalling you. Both are symptoms of anxiety.

Early Parental Loss

Black women who have experienced the early loss of a parent or parental figure are also at higher risk for the development of certain forms of anxiety. An in-depth study of Black women with panic attacks and agoraphobia conducted by Dr. Steven Friedman in New York City found that Black women were more likely to have experienced this early separation via parental divorce, parental death, or loss of contact.

At present no one seems quite sure why early parental loss may produce anxiety difficulties in adulthood. Some experts have speculated that the early loss results in a broken or insecure maternal or paternal bond that makes you more vulnerable to anxiety. Others suggest that when you lose a parent, you lose a role model, someone who shows or teaches you how to cope with various life situations. When the loss of a parent occurs early in life, it may limit your repertoire of coping skills, making you more vulnerable to panic attacks and agoraphobia.

Lily's father had two families. Although he was married to another woman and had four children, he spent Sundays with Lily and her mother. Lily adored her father and spoke to him several nights a week over the phone. When she was five, Lily's father disappeared from her life. He stopped coming over, and her phone calls were not returned. The child support checks, however, arrived on time every month. Because they lived in the same city, Lily and her mother would on occasion see him out with his family. Not once did he acknowledge their presence. At six Lily became very clingy; she did not like to be away from her mother. At sixteen Lily began having panic attacks. When she turned eighteen, she won a full scholarship to an elite small private college; she stayed one semester and then returned home to go to a local university. Now twenty-five and a college graduate, Lily still lives at home and still experiences panic attacks.

Family, genes, hormones, trauma, discrimination, stress— the causes of anxiety are many and varied. Whatever the reason, no Black woman has to go through life shackled by her anxiety difficulties. Gaining insight into the form of anxiety one is experiencing is the initial key to breaking free.

❖

TWO

Out of the Blue and Expected, Too

TEE SEEMED TO HAVE it all: a fabulous job, a beautiful home, and the admiration of thousands of women in the Houston area. Married to Keith, a man who respected and affirmed her, she had recently given birth to the couple's second child, a boy, Keith Jr., nicknamed K.J. Yesterday was K.J.'s infant dedication service. Both sets of grandparents were there as well as aunts, uncles, and godparents. Suddenly, in the midst of the ceremony, Tee's chest started to hurt and her heart began to beat fast. She couldn't seem to catch her breath, and she just knew she was dying. She looked around to signal for help, but everyone was smiling and cooing at the baby. Her mother tried to hand her the baby, but she shook her head. Her mother shot her a quizzical look but kept K.J. Somehow Tee made it through the rest of the ceremony and back to the pew. What on earth had happened? Like thousands of anxious Black women, Tee had suffered a panic attack.

WHAT IS A PANIC ATTACK?

Panic attacks are the most common manifestation of anxiety. According to the American Psychiatric Association, a panic attack is a discrete period of anxiety consisting of at least four of the following symptoms:

Increased heart rate, heart pounding
Sweating
Trembling or shaking
Going from hot to cold or cold to hot
Chest pain
Feeling as if you can't breathe, shortness of breath, or
    smothering
Feeling as if you are choking
Fear of losing control or going crazy
Feeling like you are going to die
Numbing or tingling sensations
Upset stomach or nausea
Feeling dizzy or light-headed
Feeling that this isn't really happening to you or that you
    are watching it happen

Panic attacks come in three different forms: situational, predisposed, and unexpected.

Situational and Predisposed Panic Attacks

Many Black women have panic attacks that are cued by someone, something, or some place that frightens them. My mother's good friend Willa Mae is afraid of cats. When she sees a cat, she has a panic attack. Fortunately, Willa Mae lives in the city, where cats do not roam freely. But my mother, who lives in the country, has a large garden, a henhouse, and cats. Whenever Willa Mae wanted to visit my mother, she called and let her know she was coming. My mother would gather her six children together and say, "Miss Willa Mae's on her way over." Like the Amen Corner, my siblings and I replied in unison "We know: Hide the cats." And we did. But even though she phoned before she came and even though she *knew* we spent the last half hour locking cats in the woodshed, Miss Willa Mae would park her gold Buick Electra 225 at the top of the driveway, beep the horn, roll down the window, and yell to my mother, who was standing on the front porch, "Doris, where them cats?" Only after my mother assured her the cats were locked away would Willa Mae venture out of her car onto our sidewalk.

Sometimes hiding the cats wasn't enough to prevent Willa Mae from having a panic attack. Every once in a while the thought that the cats might get out caused Willa Mae to experience a panic attack. As a child I saw it happen twice, and it wasn't pretty. A grown woman shaking, crying, and running around our yard like one of the chickens with its head cut off.

In those instances Willa Mae was experiencing what is known as a predisposed panic attack. Something about being in my mother's backyard triggered the thought that a cat was loose and resulted in a panic attack.

Women who experience cued and predisposed panic attacks suffer from phobias, which are intense irrational fears that are out of proportion to any real danger. Everyone is afraid of something, but when that fear reaches the point where it interferes with your life, it is classified as a phobia. Two categories of phobias exist: social and specific. You'll find more about social phobias in Chapter 4. Willa Mae's fear of cats is what is known as a specific phobia. My mother's cats posed no real threat to her. Truth be told, Willa Mae posed more danger to the cats.

Specific phobias—excessive fear that is triggered by a distinct person, place, or situation—and the cued and predisposed panic attacks associated with them are the most common form of anxiety exhibited by Black women. Aretha Franklin's legendary fear of flying is a specific phobia.

In her autobiography, *Aretha: From These Roots*, Ms. Franklin reveals how her specific phobia evolved. Over the course of several years, flying became increasingly stressful and uncomfortable. Initially, the physical symptoms of the cued panic attack were mild, but as time wore on, the symptoms increased in severity and duration. During a particularly difficult and bumpy flight in a prop plane from Atlanta to Detroit, Ms. Franklin experienced a full-blown panic attack. Once the plane landed, Ms. Franklin jokingly informed her manager that he wouldn't have to worry about her getting on a plane in the near future. Ms. Franklin truly believed that after a short hiatus she would resume flying. The brief break she envisioned has now lasted twenty years. In her autobiography Ms. Franklin writes, "I now realize that I should have gotten right back into it and taken another flight. I should not have let the fear get the best of me and let so much time go by."

She's right. The longer you avoid the feared situation or thing, the harder it becomes to take the first step to triumph over it. Harder, but as Aretha Franklin indicates in her book, not impossible.

It's not unusual for a woman to have more than one specific phobia. The author Bebe Moore Campbell experiences panic symptoms on planes and in elevators. In addition to cats, Miss

Willa Mae is afraid of driving over bridges. Thankfully, there were no bridges to cross to get to my parents' house, but Willa Mae's church was located across the river. The quickest route to the church was over a half-mile steel bridge that spanned the water. Until she married her second husband, who took over the driving, on Sunday mornings and Wednesday evenings Willa Mae drove fifteen miles out of her way to get to church.

The most common specific phobias that trigger cued or predisposed panic attacks for Black women are animals, heights, and enclosed places. Anxiety experts initially thought the preponderance of animal fears among Black women had a southern connection. In the early studies, many women who expressed this fear grew up or were living in southern cities or towns. More recent studies have not found a link between Black women and animal phobias and the South. Anxiety researchers have no explanation as to why so many Black women are afraid of enclosed places and heights.

Unexpected Panic Attacks

Unlike Miss Willa Mae, Aretha Franklin, or Bebe Moore Campbell, Tee's panic attacks were unexpected. This type of panic attack, which seems to come out of the blue, is the most distressing because you can't figure out what caused it. You mistakenly think that whatever you are doing at the time of the attack is the cause. Tee was drinking herbal tea when the second panic attack occurred, so she immediately stopped drinking herbal tea.

After her second panic attack, Tee began to worry that it might happen again. The worry made her nervous, afraid, and on edge. Tee played tennis twice a week for exercise and stress reduction. Several days after the second episode, Tee chased down a crosscourt shot and found herself out of breath. She began to breathe heavily and just knew she was having another panic attack. In reality she was just winded, but the sensation was so similar to that of her first panic attack that she believed she was having another one. That's what happens when you experience unexpected panic attacks: anything you do that gives you a sensation similar to that of an attack, you stop doing. Any place you go where you experience anything that seems like a panic attack, you stop going. Tee stopped playing tennis, she stopped drinking herbal tea, she stopped going to church. If her older daughter needed to be somewhere, her husband or her mother took her. Over a six-month period Tee virtually stopped going anywhere except to work. Even going there was difficult for her. Tee stopped going most places and doing most things because she was afraid of having a panic attack. This is known as agoraphobia.

Many people believe that agoraphobia is the fear of open spaces, but it is actually the fear of having a panic attack and not being able to get out or get help. Most women who experience panic attacks have a form of agoraphobia. As a result they limit the places they will go or they literally stay home. Mrs. Golden Williams, the church soloist you met in the introduction, stayed home. Her agoraphobia was severe. Tee's agoraphobia was moderate. While she avoided going most places, she was able to go to work.

Black women with cued panic attacks can also experience unexpected panic attacks. Bebe Moore Campbell suffered an unexpected panic attack in the middle of a talk she was giving at a prestigious Pennsylvania college. The attack was so unexpected and so severe that she was unable to continue. In fact, she was literally unable to speak. Concerned that their guest speaker had suffered a stroke, her hosts took her to the local hospital. The doctors kept her overnight.

YOU'D PANIC, TOO,
IF THE WITCH WAS RIDING YOU

Shauna arrived at my office one afternoon just as I was preparing to leave for home. She looked awful, as though she hadn't slept for days. She hadn't. "My cousin has you for class, and she told me I should come see you," she said. Shauna had been experiencing nocturnal panic attacks. She'd awaken from a sound sleep with her heart pounding, gasping for breath, tingling and sweating. To make matters worse, some nights just before she fell asleep her body felt as if it was paralyzed. This scared her so much that she refused to go to sleep. "Dr. Barnett," she said, "I'm afraid if I go to sleep, I'll die."

Since the earliest days of slavery, Black women have experienced unexpected panic attacks. Slave narratives tell the story of a condition known as witch riding. If you were raised in the South or raised by people who were raised in the South, you may be familiar with the term. When the witch rides you, just as you are falling asleep or just as you are waking up, you feel as if you can't move. You start seeing things that aren't there, your heart starts beating faster, you start sweating, you have trouble breathing, and you feel as if you are going to die. When the witch rides you, you have a panic attack.

As you might imagine, African-American women are loath to admit they experience witch riding. Yet those with unexpected panic attacks seem to average two or three witch-riding episodes a month. When I ask about witch riding in interviews, the women's voices drop to a whisper as they ask, "How did you know that?"

The scientific name for witch riding is "isolated sleep paralysis." A closer look at the phenomenon reveals that women of other ethnic groups and cultures report witch riding as well. However, for these women it is a once-in-a-lifetime experience that does not appear to be linked to panic attacks. Recurrent witch-riding episodes appear to be a unique feature of Black women's panic. When isolated sleep paralysis and nighttime panic attacks take place together, some Black women consider ending their lives.

SUICIDE, DEPRESSION, AND NOCTURNAL PANIC ATTACKS

Women who have these nighttime panic attacks mistake them for some type of breathing disorder or sleep apnea. Like Shauna, they become afraid of dying in their sleep. This fear is intensified when Black women suffer from nighttime panic attacks and witch riding. Imagine the terror of losing your breath and feeling paralyzed at the same time. No wonder the girl was a wreck.

Panic attacks will not kill you. No record exists of anyone dying from a panic attack or an isolated sleep paralysis episode. However, the constant fear and anxiety produced by the attacks make some women wish they were dead. As a result, some attempt suicide.

When the panic attacks and agoraphobia are at their worst, it is common for Black women to also experience depression. Depression is characterized by a sad or irritable mood most days, lasting almost all day. Depressed Black women also experience a lack of motivation, a decrease or increase in appetite, fatigue, and suicidal ideation. Black women regularly refer to depression as the blues or feeling down. Whatever name you choose to use, it is important to understand that depression is a serious problem. When panic attacks, agoraphobia, and depression happen at the same time, what often follows is a suicide attempt.

Suicide is a dirty word in most African-American communities. Remember the uproar over Ntozake Shange's play *For colored girls who have considered suicide / when the rainbow is enuf?* As Black women, the overwhelming message we receive is Black women don't kill themselves; furthermore, we are not even supposed to think about killing ourselves. Research statistics bear this out. In his report, *Mental Health: Race, Ethnicity, and Culture,* Dr. David Satcher, former Surgeon General of the United States, tells us that African-American women have the lowest suicide rate of any group in this country. When a Black woman commits suicide, little sympathy is shown for the victim. I still recall the national discussions over the suicides of newspaper columnist Leanita McClain and singer Phyllis Hyman. Instead of asking, "What caused these women so much pain that they thought death was better than life?" most Black folks asked, "Why did those light-skinned women go out and do something so stupid?" Suicide appears to be a direct violation of the Strong Black Woman code.

Although Shauna had not made a suicide attempt, she was actively thinking about it. "I'm not gonna lie, Dr. Barnett," she told me. "I have been thinking of taking myself out cuz I can't keep on like this. If I'm gonna die, I'm gonna do it on my own terms. You know what I'm saying?" Indeed, I did know. Shauna's unfamiliarity with panic attacks, coupled with her lack of sleep, had brought her to the end of her rope. Fortunately, she had sought help from her cousin, who had directed her to me. During our meeting, Shauna learned that there was a name for what was happening to her—it was called panic—and she was not alone. Shauna also learned that the lack of sleep made her more vulnerable to a depressed mood. Armed with that knowledge, she went back to her dorm room and for the first time in weeks had a good night's sleep. The next morning she scheduled an appointment at the university's psychological clinic.

PHYSICAL ILLNESS AND PANIC ATTACKS

Black women often mistake unexpected panic attacks for some type of physical illness. In the October 7, 2000, edition of *TV Guide,* actress Hattie Winston of the TV series *Becker* revealed that while visiting various college campuses with her teenage daughter, she suddenly began experiencing what she thought was a heart attack. Ms. Winston rushed to the emergency room, where the doctor told her it was "nothing but stress."

Ms. Winston's story is played out hundreds of times a day in hospital emergency rooms across this country. It's easy to do, mistake a first panic attack for a heart attack, because some similarities exist between the symptoms. According to the American Heart Association, one or more of the following are warning signals of a heart attack:

· Uncomfortable pressure, fullness, squeezing, or pain in the center of the chest lasting more than a few minutes
· Pain spreading to the shoulder, neck, or arms
· Chest discomfort with light-headedness, fainting, sweating, nausea, or shortness of breath

Chest pain, sweating, rapid heartbeat, and difficulty breathing are also symptoms associated with a panic attack. If you've never experienced either, it's likely that when the symptoms first occur, you'll think you're having a heart attack. After all, as Black women we are more familiar with heart attacks than panic attacks.

Upon receiving the doctor's diagnosis, Ms. Winston and her daughter left the hospital and went to a spa. "So I thought what every girl needs after thinking she's had a heart attack is a nice massage and facial," quipped Ms. Winston. Too bad many of us do not share her attitude. Rather than going to the spa, an action that would help relieve some of the anxiety and stress that precipitate a panic attack, we leave the hospital worried that it will happen again. Such behavior increases our fear and anxiety, making us susceptible to another panic attack.

A heart attack is not the only medical condition we confuse with a panic attack; we also confuse it with hypertension. This error frequently causes a delay in receiving effective treatment for both problems.

Black women experience hypertension at a much higher rate than any other group in this country. Hypertension leads to heart disease, stroke, and other cardiovascular diseases. Several years ago I surveyed ninety-eight women with hypertension about their anxiety levels. Eighteen of these women admitted having panic attacks, but only one told her doctor about them. When I asked the other seventeen women why they hadn't told their doctors, each gave me the same answer: "I thought it was part of the hypertension." After I gently informed them that hypertension has no outward visible symptoms, the women were stunned. "If it's not hypertension, what is it?" each asked.

Panic attacks make hypertension more difficult to treat. During a panic attack, your blood pressure increases. Some women may experience three to four panic attacks a day, which means they experience three to four spikes in blood pressure. These spikes eventually cause an elevation in your resting blood pressure rate. If you have panic attacks and hypertension, the elevations make it difficult to control your blood pressure. When I shared this information with the women, I encouraged them to tell their doctors about the panic attacks. Most did. The successful treatment of their panic attacks led to successful treatment of the hypertension. Several called to thank me. "If you hadn't told us," they said, "we would have never known."

Another common condition that is mistaken for a panic attack is hyperventilation. The fear that is produced by hyperventilation can lead you to have a panic attack. When many of us become anxious or nervous, our breathing changes. We may hold our breath, gulp for air, or begin quick and shallow breathing. All of these are forms of overbreathing, more commonly known as hyperventilation.

Hyperventilation decreases the level of carbon dioxide in the bloodstream, which in turn decreases the amount of oxygen that reaches the brain. The results are feelings of breathlessness, choking, smothering, light-headedness, and dizziness, symptoms that may be mistaken for a panic attack.

Hyperventilation may also occur during a panic attack; in fact, for many women the symptoms may overlap. Imagine how scary, distressing, and confusing it must feel to be in the midst of a panic attack and all of a sudden begin to hyperventilate.

That's what happened to Ruth. During the past five years she averaged at least one hyperventilation episode a month. These episodes usually coincided with a stressful work assignment or discussion. Ruth was so used to hyperventilating that she carried two brown paper bags in her purse at all times. Over the past six months the episodes had changed; they seemed to come out of the blue in nonstressful situations. Breathing into a bag didn't seem to help all that much, and Ruth was still left with an overwhelming sense of anxiety. She found herself dreading going to work, or anywhere else for that matter. Gradually she realized this wasn't just hyperventilation; something else was going on.

Ruth heard me being interviewed on the local 5:30 A.M. newscast. She called immediately, and as we chatted, I realized that she was hyperventilating in the midst of her panic attacks. I suggested that she contact the stress center at her local hospital for panic education classes. She did. Not only did she learn about panic attacks, but she was also taught a different way to breathe. The breathing lessons, known as breathing retraining, helped reduce the number of panic attacks and hyperventilation episodes. Today, Ruth no longer carries paper bags in her purse.

The tendency for a Black woman to mistake panic attacks for a medical problem creates a delay in receiving appropriate information and help. Even when a Black woman seeks help from a mental health professional, the combination of witch riding and panic often results in the problem being misdiagnosed. On average, Black women are seen by at least ten medical and psychological professionals before they are given the correct information, knowledge, and tools to overcome panic.

Unexpected panic attacks take ten minutes to reach their peak, but those ten minutes can change a woman's life. Confident, radiant Black women are turned into fearful, anxious girls terrified to venture out into the world. Yet there is hope and help. Thousands of Black women are living panic-free lives. Tee is, Shauna is, Ruth is, and you will, too. Unexpected panic attacks are treatable; you can reclaim your life.

◈

THREE

The "What If"s

LIKE MOST BLACK WOMEN, I come from a large ex-tended family. Each member is unique and memorable in his or her own way. But the most memorable would have to be Aunt Poo, my grandfather's youngest sister. She had been living up north for thirty years, but still retained many southern tradi-tions. She dipped snuff, she sprinkled salt over her doorways, she always had a hat on her head, and she was never without her purse. But none of those things make Aunt Poo stand out in my mind. What makes her so memorable is what happened every time anyone asked her how she was doing. "Chile," she'd reply, "I'se doing poorly." Then, before the person had a chance to respond, she would launch into a litany of all the things that were wrong or could go wrong in her life:

The weather had turned cold, and what would happen if the coal company ran out of coal and they used up all the wood in the fireplace? The price of greens had gone up ten cents, and what if they went higher? She might not be able to afford them, and she always had greens for Sunday dinner. What if the mill closed down and Silas, Aunt Poo's husband, was forced to walk the streets begging for work? What if she had to go back to work cleaning houses? She'd go on like that for ten minutes. By the time Aunt Poo got through telling you how she was doing, you were feeling poorly.

Aunt Poo was a chronic worrier. Her mind was so full of "what if"s, she could never tell you what was. She was always worried about something. Whenever we were at a family gathering and Aunt Poo was going on about her worries, Silas would gently interrupt and say, "Poo, baby, worry is a luxury Black folks can't afford."

Every once in a while at a family gathering Aunt Poo's worries would make her so tense and nervous that she made those around her tense and nervous. Sometimes it got so bad, you could feel the negativity in the air. When this happened, Silas would simply suggest it was time to leave, go get the car, and take her home. I don't know what he did when he got her home. I just know all the adults would breathe a sigh of relief when they left. Aunt Lil would say Silas had the patience of Job, and everyone would nod their head in agreement.

Aunt Poo died when I was ten. The official cause of death was heart failure, but to this day my sister, Betsey, maintains that Aunt Poo worried herself to death.

GENERALIZED ANXIETY

Women who engage in constant "what if" thinking have a generalized free-floating form of anxiety. Similar to Aunt Poo, they worry about things before they happen and after they happen. The worry is excessive, unnecessary, and has little basis in reality. This constant state of worry produces a great deal of physical and emotional tension. In fact, when you meet a Black woman with generalized anxiety, you can almost see the waves of tension and anxiety emanating from her. Aunt Poo was that way. It seemed to me that she was always in a state of constant motion. Her hands were always moving, fiddling with the buttons or safety pins on her clothing. She rarely stood still but shifted her weight from side to side, and I never saw her sit down for more than five minutes. Aunt Poo radiated nervous energy.

Women with generalized anxiety have engaged in "what if" thinking for a long time. When you ask them how long, they'll reply, "As long as they can remember." This was certainly true for Aunt Poo. Relatives who grew up with her recalled that she had always been a worrier. "Poo ain't changed in fifty years," Aunt Lil would say to anyone within earshot. "She's been this way ever since we were kids."

When you have been an excessive worrier most of your life, worrying becomes as natural as breathing. That's why, despite the family's reactions and Silas's efforts, Aunt Poo couldn't stop worrying. It was as if people were asking her to give up a part of her life. She wouldn't have known what to do if she stopped. The same is true for most women with generalized anxiety. Worry is so much a part of who they are that to ask them to simply give it up is like asking them to cut off an arm or a leg. They will refuse to do it.

DO BLACK WOMEN WORRY?

An ongoing debate among anxiety experts is whether Black women are less likely to experience generalized anxiety than other women. Black women, these experts suggest, may simply experience life in America as generalized anxiety, learn to cope with it, and continue on with their lives. Those who are not experts in anxiety espouse this same premise as well. In the controversial book *Black Macho and the Myth of the Superwoman,* author Michele Wallace writes that a Black woman does not have "the same fears, weaknesses, and insecurities as other women, but believes herself to be and is, in fact, stronger emotionally than most men."

This behavior described by psychologists and nonpsychologists alike is at the core of the definition of the Strong Black Woman. Certainly, throughout our history in America, many a Black woman, from the famous to the not so famous, has taken this approach. All the same, to suggest that being Black and female in America is synonymous with generalized anxiety and that Black women just cope with it is to build upon a stereotype and do a disservice to those who don't fit the mold.

After interviewing hundreds of Black women and surviving numerous family outings with Aunt Poo, I can say as an anxiety specialist and as a niece that Black women experience generalized anxiety. The problem is we just won't admit to worrying, and worry is the major component of generalized anxiety. Instead we will say, "It bothers me a lot" or "It concerns me a lot" or "I think about it a lot" or "I dwell on it." I've heard these statements so often, I'm beginning to wonder if there is a segment of the Black female population that has banned the word "worry" from their vocabulary.

What do Black women worry about? The answer depends on how you ask the question. You already know that if you call them worries, some Black women will deny that any exist. But when you ask about concerns or things that bother them a lot, most Black women will list the following items:

1. Money
2. Work or discrimination on the job
3. Children
4. Romantic or marital relationships
5. Housing (mortgage, adequate housing)

A Black woman with generalized anxiety worries about all these things and more; she spends an inordinate amount of time dwelling on the concerns. It is as if she has an extensive collection of "what if" tapes playing in her head of all the things that could possibly go wrong and what if everything that could go wrong did go wrong. Psychologists call these "what if" tapes catastrophic thinking. Black folks call it doom and gloom, and say, "I know she's your friend, but dag, I can't stand her negative thinking."

Whassup with Worry?

LaKeisha and LaNeisha were identical twins but were polar opposites. LaNeisha was outgoing and upbeat. LaKeisha was a worrywart. If you looked at them, you couldn't tell who was who, but when you listened to them, it was very easy to tell them apart. Now, at twenty-nine, LaKeisha's "what if" thinking has gotten so bad a rift developed in the close bond she and LaNeisha once shared. LaNeisha read about a workshop series I was doing on anxiety and persuaded LaKeisha to accompany her. "I know she's my twin and I love her, but whassup with all the worry?" complained LaNeisha "It's getting to the point that even I can't stand to be around her."

LaNeisha's question is an important one. What is up with worry? What purpose does it serve? As it turns out, a very useful one. Excessive worry allows you to avoid dealing mentally with a situation. Avoidance, whether mental or physical, is a coping mechanism, although in most cases it is not a very good one.

Countless studies have shown that when you worry, a mental action, you experience less physical arousal and expend less physical energy than you do when you actually deal with the situation. In potential anxiety-provoking situations, some women prefer the low arousal of worry to the high arousal associated with either physically fleeing or facing the situation. But there is a price to pay: Too often worry results in indecision and inaction. You are so consumed with "what if"s that you don't take the steps to make the changes you want or attempt to engage in the activities you want to engage in. As a result, you miss many opportunities and end up watching as others get the love, friendship, respect, financial security, and accolades you say you desire.

As a woman with generalized anxiety, you get caught up in a negative cycle. Seeing someone else receive what you want confirms that you were right to worry; therefore, you increase what you worry about and the amount of time you spend worrying. The more this happens, the more you worry. You fail to realize that what happened is that your worry produced indecision, which in turn produced inaction. When you sit and wait for bad things to happen, they generally won't, but neither will good things.

LaKeisha was a receptionist at a small corporation. Trained as a secretary, her secret desire was to be an administrative assistant to the corporation's vice president. The position soon became available. When the job was posted, LaKeisha immediately began to worry that she wouldn't get the position. Then she began to worry that if she got the position, she wouldn't have the skills to keep it, and if she somehow managed to hold on to the position, she wouldn't like the job. The position was given to a woman who worked in the mailroom. "See, Dr. Barnett. I told you I wouldn't get it," she said. "Yes, you did tell me that. By the way, did you apply for the position?" I asked. "No," she replied. "What would have been the point? I knew I wasn't going to get it anyway"

Worry and Depression

Worry, and the negativity that accompanies it, breeds depression. A lack of motivation and feelings of vulnerability begin to form, and when paired with indecision and inaction, they can bring your life to a standstill. Remember, women with generalized anxiety usually don't fail, they don't try. However, they misinterpret the inaction as failure. Like LaKeisha, they soon see no point in trying. Helplessness, hopelessness, and worthlessness set in.

Worry as Protection

A small but significant number of women with generalized anxiety believe worry protects them. They are convinced that if they didn't worry, bad things would happen. Excessive worry for these women serves the same purpose as a lucky rabbit's foot.

In my teens and twenties, I was actively involved in the theater. I did it for fun, but several women involved in the company were extremely serious about it. One of these women, Jill, was a chronic worrier. One of the many things she worried about was acting. She worried from the time auditions were announced to the time the curtain rose on opening night. It was difficult acting with Jill. On stage she was brilliant, but offstage her worry and tension made other actors want to slap her—I must admit the thought did cross my mind a time or two. No one ever did; they just talked about her. Jill went on to develop a respectable professional career in regional theater. Recently I ran into her in Chicago. As we chatted about our careers and families, Jill said, "Remember how everyone used to talk about how much I worried?" "Yes," I replied. "Well, in a sense, if it wasn't for worry, I wouldn't be where I am today. But sometimes I wonder how much further I'd be if I didn't worry."

Worry and Physical Illness

Contrary to my sister Betsey's belief, worry did not kill Aunt Poo, and there are no documented cases of any Black woman worrying herself to death. Worry can, however, make you sick. Indeed, most women first seek help for the physical discomfort that is partly created by generalized anxiety, rather than the worry itself.

Most physical disorders associated with generalized anxiety occur in the stomach region and include ulcers and irritable bowel syndrome. Ulcers are sores or holes in the lining of the stomach or the beginning of the small intestine. Excessive worry does not create an ulcer; new research has shown that a bacterium creates ulcers. However, worry and the inaction associated with it may make an ulcer worse. Worrying about all the possible diseases an ulcer might be can create a delay in seeking a diagnosis. The possibility exists that generalized anxiety and the behaviors associated with it may place you at higher risk to contract the bacterium that causes ulcers.

Irritable bowel syndrome (IBS) is an illness that may not be familiar to many of you even though it is a fairly common disorder that involves gas pain, bloating, constipation, or diarrhea. In severe cases, individuals experience an emptying of their bowels or incontinence. As you can imagine, many women with IBS are reluctant to interact socially, fearing that they may not be able to find a restroom quickly.

The pain and embarrassment caused by IBS often increase the amount of worry and anxiety women experience. So much attention is given to the symptoms of the disorder that many women neglect to mention the free-floating anxiety and worry that are also taking place. To their credit, more and more physicians are aware of the relationship between IBS and generalized anxiety, and are routinely assessing for this anxiety difficulty among women who come in with irritable bowel problems.

Mavis was voted the girl most likely to have an ulcer at twenty-one by her high school class. At twenty-five she was a nervous wreck. Recently she began to experience severe stomach pains and felt bloated and gassy. What if she was pregnant? What if she had cancer? What if it was something worse? These worries ran through her mind. She spent so much time dwelling on what it could be that she never went to a doctor to find out what it was. Then she doubled over in pain in the checkout line of the grocery store. The manager called the paramedics, and they rushed her to the emergency room. There she was diagnosed with irritable bowel syndrome. When the doctor explained the diagnosis, Mavis began to worry. About the health insurance: "What if my insurance won't cover the hospital costs?" she asked the nurse. The groceries: "What if the store charges me for all that food?" she said to no one in particular. The diagnosis: "What if I don't get better?" she asked the doctor. After the third "what if" statement, the doctor screened for generalized anxiety. Mavis met all the criteria.

Women with generalized anxiety frequently experience headaches. In a sense, they worry so hard, their head hurts. Physicians often call these tension headaches and encourage women to eliminate stress from their lives. In reality, these headaches are created by the free-floating anxiety, physical tension, and worry that are part of generalized anxiety. Therefore, reducing your "stress level" will not reduce your headaches, but reducing the amount of time you spend worrying will cause a decrease in headaches.

Trina called me after reading my column, "Focus on the Mind," in the local Black newspaper. She'd experienced headaches ever since she was a teenager. She was also a chronic worrier. As an adult she had seen several specialists, but no amount of medication or stress-reduction techniques seemed to help. Over the past five years the headaches seemed to increase in intensity. In the past six months she had missed twenty-four days of work because the pain was so severe. Her supervisor had written her up for taking so much time off. A thorough assessment revealed that she experienced generalized anxiety. Working with a neurologist, Trina and I put together an education and treatment program that combined medication, therapy, and meditation. Within three months Trina's worrying and her headaches began to subside. Last month Trina missed one day of work, and it wasn't because of a headache.

Worry will wear you out. The act of worrying is mentally fatiguing. At the same time, worry makes you restless, so while you're fatigued, you also can't sleep, making the fatigue worse. If you've ever gone to bed with something weighing on your mind, you know what I'm talking about. You can't sleep, you toss and turn, or you wake up with the problem on your mind and can't get back to sleep. For this reason women with generalized anxiety often ask their doctors for "a little something to help me sleep." If the physician fails to recognize the worry component, she may prescribe sleeping pills and encourage the patient to reduce the stress in her life. The prescription and advice, though well intentioned, do not address the real problem.

LaKeisha had been experiencing sleep problems for quite some time. In the beginning, her doctor prescribed a mild sedative to be taken as needed. LaKeisha exhausted the prescription in three weeks. Her doctor refused to refill the prescription; instead, she referred LaKeisha to a psychiatrist to discuss "what was really bothering her." LaKeisha never went, and her sleep problems grew worse, got better, and then grew worse again. By the time she and LaNeisha enrolled in the workshop, she was getting only three to four hours of sleep a night.

Should I Just Accept It?

Because many women have lived with the worry, tension, and physical symptoms of generalized anxiety for so long, they often wonder if instead of seeking help for the problem, they should just learn to live with it. That's what my Aunt Poo did, in part because back in those days generalized anxiety disorder did not exist as a diagnostic category, so no one could tell her that help was available and she didn't have to live that way. That's what LaKeisha did, until LaNeisha got to the point where she couldn't stand it and found out help was available. Although LaNeisha accompanied her to the workshops, it wasn't until LaKeisha decided she didn't want to be anxious for the rest of her life that a change began to take place.

HOPE

You can learn to manage generalized anxiety to the point where the excessive worry, tension, and physical symptoms lessen or disappear. Because most women have engaged in the pattern of worry for many years, the likelihood exists that they will slip back into that old pattern and the generalized anxiety will reappear. That's why I believe it is important to think about generalized anxiety as a chronic difficulty similar to hypertension.

As most of you are aware, once you get your hypertension under control, if you fall back into certain habits—such as eating salty and high-fat foods, cutting back on your exercise, or taking on more and more stressful assignments or jobs—the hypertension will return. The same is true for generalized anxiety. If you want to remain free of excessive worry and tension, you must continue to practice and do all the things that got you to that point originally. And if you have a setback—and most women occasionally have a setback—you must recognize it for what it is, a temporary condition, and move forward. If you keep this in mind, using the techniques and resources discussed later in this book you will soon find that excessive worry no longer rules your life.

FOUR

What Must Other People Think?

Y ESTERDAY THE MOST AMAZING thing happened in
church. It all started when the minister of music lost her
wig. No, I don't mean she got the Holy Spirit and knocked her
wig askew. I mean the wig fell off her head and hit the floor. Here
is what happened: The choir was in the throes of singing "No
Never Alone." Sister Bea, minister of music, reared back her
head to hit a high note, and the wig slid off. Girlfriend didn't
miss a beat. She finished the song and did an encore, and when
that was over, she bent down, picked up the wig, waved it at the
congregation, and sat down . . . wigless. At that moment Sister
Maya turned to me and whispered, "I wish I could be like Sister
Bea," she said. "Wigless?" I replied. "No," she said. "Unafraid.
Do you think," she whispered, "you could help me become a bit
more like her? A little less afraid of what people might think?"

I turned my full attention to Sister Maya. She was a tall,
beautiful, soft-spoken woman with both an M.B.A. and a law
degree from Harvard. Yet Maya had toiled in the same lowly assistant professor position at the law school for ten years. She

hadn't been promoted, and despite the fact that she was a skill-ful interpreter of the tax law, she hadn't written anything in years. She wanted to get married, but in the five years I had known her, she had never gone out with anyone more than twice. Some people thought Maya was stuck-up; other people thought she was stuck in a rut. That morning in church I real-ized she was neither: Maya was paralyzed by fear. She didn't write because she was afraid people wouldn't like what she wrote. She didn't try for promotion because she was afraid she wouldn't get it. She didn't go out with anyone because she was afraid they wouldn't like her.

Maya's fear has a name: social anxiety. Women with this form of anxiety are afraid of being embarrassed or humiliated in social or other situations. They fear they will do the wrong thing, say the wrong thing, or look the wrong way in the situa-tion and be negatively evaluated by others. This fear is often so intense that women will experience a cued panic attack in the social situation. Just the thought of engaging in the social be-havior can produce a predisposed panic attack. For these rea-sons social anxiety is sometimes called social phobia. Women with social anxiety recognize the fear is unreasonable or exces-sive but feel helpless to change the situation.

LIMITED AND GENERALIZED SOCIAL ANXIETY

Socially anxious Black women exhibit this difficulty in ei-ther a limited or a generalized manner. In limited social anxiety, a woman's anxiety and fear are confined to one or two social situations such as public speaking, dating, signing a contract or credit/debit card slip in public, or dancing, eating, or perform-ing in public. The woman who does everything in her power to avoid taking the high school or college speech class is a classic example of limited social anxiety. With the generalized version, anxiety and fear are experienced in almost every social situation. Regardless of the variety, socially anxious Black women either avoid social situations or endure them under great duress.

Social Anxiety—The Limited Version

Maya's social anxiety was limited in nature, revolving around the areas of dating and evaluation of her written work by others in her field. At one point she wrote and published articles. In fact, an article written five years ago was published in a prestigious journal and awarded a prize. At that point many considered her a rising star in the field. But several leading tax law scholars criticized the prize-winning article, one going so far as to insinuate that the article was being heralded because of the race of its author, not its content. Maya was mortified and humiliated. She vowed her next article would be so good that no one would criticize it and her race would be a nonissue. She'd spent the last five years working on the same two articles. Every time she was ready to publish one of them, she'd find something she feared would be criticized and continued to work on it some more. As a result, the articles remained unpublished.

This fear of negative evaluation directly affected her ability to be promoted. To be promoted at the law school you had to publish. Maya's articles remained in her file drawer, unpublished, and therefore Maya could not be promoted.

Maya has a warm brown complexion and is a beautiful woman, but she doesn't think so. As a child her caramel-colored, red-haired older brothers teased her about being dark and ugly. The feelings of humiliation and embarrassment connected with her skin tone remained with her into adulthood. When a man asked her out, she was terrified that he would reject her because she was too dark. Rather than suffer the humiliation of being rejected, she broke it off.

Women with the limited form of social anxiety often perform well in other social situations. In other areas, Maya was confident. Law students consistently raved about her classes, and her teaching evaluations were among the highest. Colleagues who worked in law firms called her in to consult on difficult tax law cases and raved about her knowledge. Many organizations asked her to be the guest speaker at their banquets. She enjoyed doing these things and did them well. But Maya wanted to publish and she wanted to date; she just wasn't willing to risk the anxiety and rejection.

Social Anxiety—The Generalized Version

Janise was terrified that other Black women would think she "acted white." The girls in high school had said that about her, and she felt as if none of the Black kids really liked her. During high school her feelings of being rejected by other Black students reached the point where she started experiencing panic attacks whenever another Black teen approached her. The situation became so bad she began carrying a sipper bottle filled with vodka and coke. Every time she thought one of the Black kids was going to say something to her, she took a sip. It calmed her nerves.

Now that she was in college, she wasn't going to let that happen again. So what if she thought Lil' Kim demeaned Black women; she wasn't going to let her new friends know that. So what if she thought the White girl next door was fun; she wasn't going to make friends with her. She was going to be the type of Black woman that other Black women would want as a friend. The problem was that she was so busy being what she thought other people wanted her to be, she forgot to be herself. This made her more anxious and miserable than she had been in high school.

"I've always thought of myself as Black and take great pride in the history of our people," said Janise. "When in my freshman year of high school the Black kids began to say that I acted white, it was just like something inside me died. I never, ever want to feel that way again. I felt like everything I did was ridiculed. The white kids weren't much better. I remember several of them saying, 'But gee, Janise, you don't act like a Black girl.' What was that supposed to mean? Whether I am with Blacks or Whites I feel like I'm walking this tightrope—one false move and it'll be high school all over again. The vodka helps, but I don't want to turn into an alcoholic."

Janise's fear of being accused of acting white affected almost all her social situations. Regardless of whether she was interacting with Blacks or Whites, Janise found herself not wanting to do anything that would make either group think she wasn't behaving as they thought a Black woman should behave and face rejection and humiliation. To prevent a repeat of her high school experience, she began acting like someone she knew wasn't her, once again using vodka to ease the physical symptoms of her anxiety.

Whitney's Terrible, Horrible, Very Bad Middle School Incident

Every Black woman who knew her disliked Whitney. They found her shallow and self-absorbed. She took the slightest thing as criticism and responded in a hostile way to the individual responsible. It got to the point where she wouldn't speak to other women. If her hair wasn't done or her designer clothes weren't dry-cleaned, she didn't go out. Everything she did had to be perfect, or she wouldn't do it. Being perfect, she reasoned, would make people like her. It had the opposite effect.

Whitney's social anxiety took the form of anger and hostility. The anger and hostility were ways to prevent people from criticizing her. She would cut them off before they could say anything negative. The problem was people weren't going to be critical or say negative things to her; she just perceived it that way. Her hostility made people shun her. When Whitney said women didn't like her, she was pretty much telling the truth.

Like thousands of other socially anxious women, Whitney was able to identify the exact moment her social phobia began. Her father had worked his way up from the steel mills of Pennsylvania to owning his own corporation and a prominent place in Black and White society. From an early age her mother impressed upon her the need to always look and behave perfectly. If she looked or behaved badly, it would reflect unfavorably on her father. Other people were just looking for the opportunity to tear her family down—crabs in a barrel, her mother called them. Her mother also warned her to watch out for girls who wanted to be her friend only because her father was rich.

One day in sixth grade Whitney stood up in class, the zipper on her skirt broke, and the garment fell to the floor. Whitney quickly pulled it up, grateful that no one had seen what had happened, or so she thought. Just then a girl she considered her friend said in a voice loud enough for everyone to hear, "Ooh, Whitney's skirt fell off. I guess her rich daddy can't buy her skinny yellow behind clothes that fit." The entire room started laughing. The teacher made the girl apologize, but for Whitney the damage had been done. The image of the entire class laughing at her was one she would never forget.

Two days later Whitney wore a very pretty outfit to school. When another girl complimented her on the outfit, Whitney remembered that she had been among those laughing at her. She began to recall the embarrassment and humiliation of two days ago, her heart began to beat a little faster, and she began to feel tense and anxious. Certain the girl was going to make fun of her, Whitney brushed past her without speaking. The girl thought Whitney was being unfriendly and stuck-up. In reality, Whitney was protecting herself from what she thought was going to be another humiliating incident. She would not be embarrassed again; it was simply too painful. She would snub others before they snubbed her.

What happened after the "terrible, horrible, very bad" incident was just as important for Whitney as the original incident itself. The memory of the other kids' laughter and comments, coupled with the emotions and physical sensations their behavior produced, carried over into similar social situations. She became tense, afraid, and convinced that others were going to say something negative about her appearance, her clothing, or both. In fact, she expected it.

The psychologist William James said, "If you expect a thing to become so, and you expect and believe it long enough and hard enough, it will become so." Whitney's expectations led to the misinterpretation of others' actions, behaviors, and motives. Thus, her expectations of being negatively seen by others were met. This was distressing to Whitney. She wanted friends, women to shop with, laugh with, and share secrets with, but the memory of the horrible incident combined with her mother's warnings and her own anxiety and fear just kept getting in the way.

SOCIAL ANXIETY AND THE BLACK EXPERIENCE
Twice as Good, Half as Far

The stories of Maya, Janise, and Whitney illustrate how issues related to being a Black woman in America may complicate social anxiety. From the cradle many of us are told and come to believe that Black women have to be *twice as good to go half as far.* Early on, we come to understand that our success is not our own but reflects positively on all Black Americans. Maya was taught and strongly believed these things; therefore, when her prize-winning article was sharply criticized and her race was raised as an issue, the anxiety and humiliation she felt was twofold: individually for herself, and collectively for Black women. Experiencing those emotions on a dual level heightened Maya's sense of inadequacy and fear of her scholarly work being negatively evaluated.

Gena, a friend of Maya's as well as a civil rights professor at the same law school, used her "twice as good, half as far" and "representing the race" beliefs to buffer her response to criticism. Rather than feeling embarrassed when her articles were criticized or her race was raised as an issue, Gena saw it for what it was: part of the law school culture and prejudice. She told herself, "Everyone's articles get criticized. I expected this. I also know that I am more likely to be criticized because of my race. If I let it get to me, stop me from doing my best, I am letting prejudice win." The difference between the two women's approaches appears directly related to how they interpret and handle discrimination and prejudice, and the amount of stress and other anxiety risk factors present in their lives.

Acting White

Acting white is one of the most negative criticisms young Black women can hurl at one another. Countless numbers of young women have questioned their behavior, attitudes, and beliefs after hearing this accusation. An important part of being an adolescent is finding out who you are and what you believe in, separate and apart from your parents. Psychologists refer to this as establishing your own social identity. For Black teens a central part of that identity is their racial identity, determining for themselves what it means to be Black and the value they place on that meaning. When the other teens said she acted white, Janise felt as if they were rejecting her and attacking the core of her identity. Janise began to expect rejection from other Black students. As a result, whenever another Black student approached her or she was in social situations with other Black students, she began to experience panic symptoms. That's why she used the vodka; the alcohol helped steady her nerves.

Soft-spoken and somewhat shy, as a college student Janise was acting like someone she wasn't and was terrified that someone would find out the truth. What would happen if they actually found out what she really thought and believed? Janise didn't want to be white, she just wanted to be herself; but given her high school experience, she was afraid if she did so, she wouldn't have any friends. The panic attacks returned, and once again she began using the vodka, this time hiding it in an insulated coffee cup.

An extremely interesting finding from my work with socially anxious Black women is that most make reference to being accused of acting white in either junior high/middle school or high school. Over half report that they still hear that accusation in some form or fashion now that they are adults. Understanding the accusation of acting white may be important in understanding how social anxiety develops in some Black women. Specifically, in Janise's case, fear of being accused of acting white appears to have combined with her natural shyness to produce social anxiety.

Shyness

Psychologists Lynn Henderson and Phillip Zimbardo, co-directors of the Shyness Institute, describe shyness as discomfort or inhibition in interpersonal situations that interferes with one's personal or professional goals. At some point in our lives all of us have experienced a mild episode of shyness. We have found ourselves tongue-tied in the presence of an attractive member of the opposite sex, or our normal voice was reduced to a whisper when we were asked a question in a roomful of people.

Shyness's role in the development of social anxiety is often misunderstood. Simply being shy does not mean you are socially anxious. While some shy people develop social anxiety, others do not. Socially anxious women are what psychologists Gregory and Barbara Markway describe as "painfully shy." I like that term because it accurately describes what it is like for many Black women whose social anxiety extends to almost all social situations. The level of psychological distress and discomfort is so intense it literally hurts. Some women with generalized social anxiety avoid new social situations altogether. They in effect become social avoidants.

In the April 8, 1996, issue of *Jet* magazine, several Black psychologists suggested that what is interpreted as shyness, particularly in the presence of Whites, is actually an appropriate and adaptive coping strategy for Blacks known as mask wearing. Remember these lines from Paul Laurence Dunbar's poem "We Wear the Mask":

We wear the mask that grins and lies,
It hides our cheeks and shades our eyes—
This debt we pay to human guile;
With torn and bleeding hearts we smile,
And mouth with myriad subtleties.

Why should the world be overwise,
In counting all our tears and sighs?
Nay, let them only see us, while
    We wear the mask.

In other words, quiet, reticent behavior allows African Americans to hide their true feelings from the world.

Some psychologists suggest that shyness is not a trait generally found among Black women. These experts subscribe to the notion that "a Black woman will tell you in no uncertain terms what she thinks." While we all know Black women like this, we should not take it as evidence that shyness is a rare trait among Black women. In fact, Black women are just as likely as women of other races to be shy.

Skin Color

Skin color issues remain intertwined with perceptions of appearance in some Black communities. As Maya's and Whitney's stories confirm, appearance is a major source of social anxiety for Black women. Skin color is a visible part of a Black woman's appearance. When we describe a Black woman to another Black person, we frequently include a description of skin tone. Socially anxious women tend to see themselves through the eyes of others rather than through their own eyes. Maya is a beautiful woman, yet she sees herself and believes others see her as dark and ugly. This is a direct result of the evaluation she was constantly given as a child and which she internalized. Whitney still sees herself through the eyes of her sixth-grade classmates: the girl with the rich daddy whose skirt fell off, exposing her skinny yellow behind. Neither seems to realize that age, maturity, and new observers change these perceptions. It is as if Maya's and Whitney's perceptions of self are stuck in time. Each still sees herself as she believes others saw her twenty to thirty years ago. The fact that these self-perceptions are tinged by the skin color issue makes them harder to erase from one's memory.

Historically, skin color has influenced African-American women's social status. Family histories and the biographies and autobiographies of African Americans, as well as history books, are replete with stories about being denied or afforded certain social, educational, and economic opportunities because of light or dark skin. Prior to the civil rights movement, certain professions were closed to dark-skinned women. Membership in certain churches, clubs, and sororities was often based on skin tone. Light-skinned women were more likely to marry high-status Black males, granting them access to the Black middle class. Although the social divisions between dark and light have narrowed considerably, some vestiges still remain.

Brenda Payton, in a column for the *Oakland Tribune,* tells the story of a dark-skinned female friend who every time she attends a social gathering of African Americans calculates the number of light- and dark-skinned Blacks in the room. By doing so, her friend can ascertain whether it is a dark- or light-skinned gathering. Confident her friend is simply obsessed with color, Payton tries her friend's calculation at several parties she attends. She is surprised by her findings. Her friend seems to be correct: Socially, we still seem to segregate ourselves along skin color lines.

Skin color also affects one of the most telling symptoms of embarrassment: blushing. When speaking or writing about social anxiety, various anxiety experts will relate how, when embarrassed, women actually turn red as a beet. As Black women the richness of our skin tones makes blushing an unlikely occurrence except for those with very light skin. We are more likely to feel our cheeks grow warm, a sensation that cannot be seen by others.

OTHER PEOPLE'S STANDARDS

In a pivotal scene from the movie *The Best Man,* henpecked lawyer turned youth worker Murch, played by Harold Perrineau Jr., tells stripper/college student Candy, portrayed by Regina Hall, "If you don't define yourself for yourself, you'll be crushed into other people's fantasies for you and eaten alive." Actually, Murch is quoting the poet and writer Audre Lorde. As an anxiety expert I find it is one of my favorite quotes because it accurately depicts what happens to socially anxious Black women. Rather than defining your own standards for who you are and what you believe, you define yourself by what you envision other people's standards to be. The problem is these standards you think up are so harsh that you stagger under the weight. As Maya so aptly put it, "What I think other people think is far worse than what they are actually thinking."

Janise and Whitney were also guilty of thinking this way. Until she sought help, Janise truly believed other Blacks judged her for who she wasn't, rather than on her merits. As for Whitney, her fear that others would see her as less than perfect affected just about every facet of her life.

BEING ON HIGHEST ALERT

Maya's, Janise's, and Whitney's social behaviors are linked together by a common characteristic, hypervigilance, which is the psychological equivalent of being on highest alert. In this state you look for any sign that others are negatively evaluating you or that you are about to be embarrassed or humiliated. What triggers this state is the common belief that something about you is unacceptable to other people. When this belief is paired with the tendency to judge using other people's standards, a state of hypervigilance emerges.

In this state of highest alert, your attention is drawn to the slightest indication that another person sees you negatively. Furthermore, you have a harder time refocusing your attention on something more positive. You misinterpret the words, behaviors, and looks of others in such a way that they confirm your fears of rejection, humiliation, or embarrassment. You fail to consider an alternative reason for the other person's actions or reactions. That's the other piece of being socially anxious and hypervigilant: Your focus tends to be inward, on yourself. You believe everyone is as focused on your imperfections as you are. *This self-focus is different from being self-absorbed.* Trust me, most divas are not socially anxious.

Maya believed she was too dark and men didn't really want to date her. One time on a date she caught the man looking at her intently. She abruptly ended the evening and asked him to take her home. He was looking at her intently not because, as Maya believed, she was too dark, but because she was so lovely. Maya's state of hypervigilance resulted in her misinterpreting the meaning of the gentleman's gaze, causing her to end a relationship before it ever began.

In high school Janise's hypervigilance reached the point where she didn't even wait for the other person to speak. If a Black student approached her and wasn't smiling, she took it as a sign that the individual was getting ready to say something nasty to her, and she took a drink. If the student approached her and was smiling, she took that as a sign the student was going to make fun of her, and she took a drink. In most cases she perceived negative intent when none existed.

As for Whitney, being in a state of highest alert increased her hostility toward other women. She went into social situations looking for the worst from other women, and usually found it. Interestingly, if she didn't look so hard for it, she never would have found it.

SOCIAL ANXIETY AND OTHER DIFFICULTIES
Depression

Being socially anxious may create other problems. Like Maya, Janise, and Whitney, many socially anxious Black women want social interaction, they want friends and significant others. When relationships do not pan out and these women continuously avoid social interactions, they may begin to experience great sadness regarding their situation. When negative self-evaluation and a sense of despair are also present, women with social anxiety develop depression.

Alcohol

Janise used vodka to ease her anxiety symptoms and help her get through various social situations. It calmed her nerves. Alcohol use is a fairly common practice among women with social anxiety. Alcohol lowers inhibitions. Some women believe alcohol relaxes them; others swear alcohol makes them more witty; still others think it gives them the courage to face difficult social situations. Whatever the reason, these women come to rely on alcohol and develop a drinking problem. Glenda, the young woman in detox, is a prime example. Drinking made her less anxious and calmed her nerves when she was out with friends, but as time went on, it took more and more alcohol— until she was falling out in the streets, dead drunk.

Alcohol is readily available in most social situations. Some of us believe that if a party, wedding, dinner, or dance doesn't have alcohol, we are not going to have a good time. Statistics from the hospitality industry bear this out: People stay longer at social events where alcohol is served than they do at events where alcohol is not served. Given this fact, alcohol and social situations seem to go together, and it is not surprising that a portion of socially anxious Black women develop alcohol problems.

HOPE

Whether you are experiencing limited or generalized social anxiety, you can learn to overcome your fear. Because you are dealing with only one or two specific social situations, treating the limited version requires less time than treating the generalized version. With the generalized version you are dealing not only with anxiety but also with a negative sense of self, the be-

lief that something about you does not measure up to other people. For this reason a woman with social anxiety must learn to
change what she believes about herself. She must cast aside
those images of middle school and high school and replace them
with the image of who she is today and who she wants to become. Changing these images and beliefs takes time, but you
can change them. I see it happen every day as I watch women
steadily take steps to erase social anxiety from their lives.

Yesterday, the most amazing thing happened in church. Sister Maya took the first step to overcoming social anxiety: She
asked for help.

WHEN I WAS SEVENTEEN, one of my favorite people was Honey Mills. She was five feet tall, 110 pounds, impeccably dressed, and always draped in rubies, emeralds, or opals. As far as Miss Honey was concerned, diamonds were common. Prior to marrying Mr. Mills, Miss Honey had led a colorful life. She had been, among other things, a jazz singer, a dairy farmer, and a bootlegger's mistress, and later she became a state senator. In short, Miss Honey was a diva before the world had heard of Aretha, Whitney, or Miss Ross.

Miss Honey was fascinating. Even more fascinating was Miss Honey's house. It contained the largest collection of books I had ever seen. Miss Honey owned multiple copies of each book. Her favorite activity was shopping. Every Saturday she and her daughter, Annie, would go to flea markets, consignment stores, or auctions, and come back with all kinds of treasures. On one of their trips Miss Honey bought the entire contents of a Black beauty shop that had gone out of business. While everyone else had either a dryer with a hood or a hot plate and a straightening comb, Annie had an entire beauty salon at her disposal. And somewhere between the summers of my seventeenth and twenty-second years, Miss Honey found a tour bus at the flea market and persuaded Annie to drive it home.

The years passed. Annie got married and Mr. Mills passed away. When I'd returned home from college, graduate school, or my internship, it seemed to me that Miss Honey was accumulating more and more stuff. But I was away for long periods of time, and what seemed abnormal to me didn't seem to bother anyone else. When I was thirty-five, I received a phone call from my sister. "Angie," she said, "Miss Honey's dead." I was shocked; even more shocking was the story my sister told of how Miss Honey had died.

That morning Annie and her mother were scheduled to go shopping. When Annie pulled into the driveway, Miss Honey wasn't outside. She knocked and called her name, but Miss Honey didn't respond. When Annie put her key in the lock, the door wouldn't open. She called 911. The police, the fire department, the paramedics, and the neighbors responded. She called my sister and my mother. The fire department arrived, broke a window, and was immediately confronted by stacks and rows of boxes, books, papers, and suitcases. It took the emergency team a half hour to find Miss Honey. Then it took them an hour to remove her from the home because they had to clear a path. Annie was hysterical, the neighbors were hysterical, and the fire captain was mad. "I would never allow my mother to live in such a mess," he said. "For crying out loud, there's a tour bus in the front yard. Didn't that tell you people anything?" The crowd did not appreciate his assessment. Just when it looked as if more than one life would be lost that day, my mother stepped forward, grabbed the fire captain by his lapels, and said in her "pillar of the community" voice, "That will be quite enough. Everybody has their little idiosyncrasies."

For the first time in a very long time my mother was wrong. Miss Honey wasn't idiosyncratic; she was anxious. Her anxiety manifested itself in what is known as compulsive hoarding, a form of obsessive-compulsive disorder (also called OCD). Buying and accumulating stuff helped her feel less anxious. The problem was the anxiety would quickly return, and she would have to buy and accumulate more and more stuff to make it go away.

The anxiety associated with OCD is caused by thoughts that keep repeating themselves in your head. Like a broken record or scratched CD, they literally get stuck. These repetitive thoughts are known as obsessions. Psychiatrist Judith Rappaport says obsessions are like having hiccups in your brain. It's a wonderful analogy; just like hiccups, obsessions are difficult to get rid of, annoying, and unwanted. Common obsessions include thoughts of contamination or germs; thoughts that if you behave in a certain way, you will cause harm to someone; inappropriate sexual thoughts; and sin. Some people confuse repetitive thoughts with hearing voices inside your head. Whereas the content of an obsession is unusual, annoying, or doesn't make a lot of sense, it is a thought. Voices are hallucinations and are not a symptom of anxiety but of a very serious psychological disturbance.

To gain relief from the anxiety and distress produced by the obsessions—in other words, to try to get the thoughts unstuck—women begin to engage in some sort of physical or mental behavior that they keep doing over and over again. These repetitive behaviors are known as compulsions. Common compulsions include washing, cleaning, checking, counting, and praying. Most women do not want to engage in the compulsions but are extremely frightened about what will happen if they stop the repetitive behavior. They believe a catastrophe will occur if they do not engage in the behavior. Over time, the repetitive behaviors become more elaborate and take on a ritualistic quality. For example, a behavior may have to occur at bedtime or after waking up, when leaving the house or before sitting down, every hour on the hour or until it feels right.

Compulsions offer temporary relief from the anxiety produced by obsessive thoughts, but the repetitive thoughts always seem to return; the anxiety and distress increase, and the compulsions begin again. The whole process becomes a vicious cycle of anxiety buildup and anxiety reduction, with many women spending a good portion of their day engaging in the repetitive thoughts and behaviors pattern.

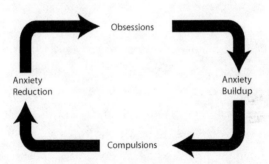

Obsessions

Anxiety
Reduction

Anxiety
Buildup

Compulsions

I don't know what obsessive thoughts bothered Miss Honey. What I do know is the anxiety and distress caused by these thoughts resulted in the compulsion to collect and hoard things and never being able to throw anything away. The greater her anxiety and distress, the more she hoarded. Her daughter's marriage and Mr. Mills's death left her by herself. The loneliness increased her stress level and shortened her anxiety buildup–anxiety reduction cycle. At the time of her death Miss Honey was probably in a constant state of hoarding.

Miss Honey hid her OCD by visiting. Rather than have people in, she was always out. She was always visiting people or holding political meetings at other people's houses. When Annie went to the house to pick her up to go shopping or to another event, Miss Honey would be waiting on the front porch. She kept the condition and contents of the inside of her home a secret from everyone, including her own daughter.

After her mother's death, as Annie gained insight into OCD, she wanted to share her knowledge with the Black community. Perhaps, she reasoned, she might be able to help someone else whose mother or father engaged in such behavior. But when she tried to tell others about her mother and OCD, no one wanted to listen. Worse, people began to view her as either the ungrateful daughter who was disrespectful of her dead mother or the bereaved daughter who was so grief-stricken that she was talking some nonsense about a disorder when everybody knew Miss Honey was a diva who just went a little overboard with the flea marketing.

Annie's experience reflects the Black community's unfamiliarity with OCD and its unwillingness to accept the fact that Black women would engage in such behavior. Whenever I speak about the disorder, the first question from the audience is "Black women get this?" Not only do we get it, we tend to get it more often than any other group of people in this country. We also tend to suffer from OCD longer than any other group. When it comes to our emotional health, Black women are champion secret keepers. We are so afraid that no one will understand or that others will think we are crazy that we choose not to say a word about the obsessive thoughts and repetitive behaviors—even to professionals who could help us. It is as if Black women have been programmed to believe it doesn't matter what anyone calls us as long as they don't call us crazy.

THE PRAYER WARRIOR

Rosalie was usually the first person to arrive at church on Sunday morning and the last person to leave on Sunday night. As the leader of the congregation's prayer team, she was faithful in showing up at the church Monday through Friday for her 6:30 to 7:30 A.M. prayer slot. Behind her back, several church members claimed she wore out the pews, praying and fasting. Others considered her one of the saints of the church. In reality, Rosalie felt like one of the congregation's biggest sinners. She was constantly bothered by repetitive thoughts that she had sinned and was damned to hell. Prayer and fasting provided temporary relief.

Rosalie let people believe she was a prayer warrior rather than admit she was at war with prayer. This form of OCD is known as scrupulosity and involves obsessions and compulsions that are religious in nature. Obsessions common to this form of OCD include the belief you have committed an unpardonable sin or that your sins have not been forgiven. This element of unbelief has led some psychologists to label scrupulosity the doubting form of OCD. Excessive praying, chanting, candle lighting, and religious self-punishment are common compulsions associated with scrupulosity.

Some anxiety professionals have suggested that scrupulosity is the form of OCD most prevalent among Black women. Although I cannot say for certain whether it is or not, what I do know is that whether we worship God, Jehovah, Allah, Oshun, or Isis, spirituality is a core element of the Black female personality. Therefore, compulsions that are part of our spiritual traditions are easy to hide from friends, family, and spiritual leaders. Search your memory. When was the last time you heard anyone tell a Black woman she prayed too much?

MISS CLEAN

Rachel's friends claimed she always ran on CP time and never met a bathroom mirror she didn't like. In reality, Rachel experienced repetitive thoughts of contamination that resulted in cleaning and hand-washing compulsions. Some days she couldn't leave her apartment until she felt it had been decontaminated. Sometimes this took one or two extra hours; other times it took all day.

Once during a friend's Super Bowl party she spent an hour in the bathroom washing her hands. None of the men noticed, but several women asked her what she was doing in there. She played it off by laughing, and didn't give them an answer. Rachel's hands were so chapped and full of hangnails that she went to see a dermatologist. He was able to provide some relief from the chapping but not for the obsessions and compulsions. You see, Rachel never told him about her constant need to wash and clean.

KEEPING SECRETS

Keeping obsessions and compulsions a secret comes at a great emotional, financial, and spiritual cost. The secret keeper is constantly worried that someone will find out. She doesn't apply for jobs or loses jobs because she doesn't want people to know about her problem. She lies to others; more important, she lies to herself about what is really happening. Her efforts to keep the repetitive thoughts and behaviors a secret breed shame, guilt, and dishonesty. Her distress level rises, causing an increase in her obsessions and compulsions. She begins to feel angry, hopeless, or both, and gives in to the OCD on a daily basis.

Rachel saw her dermatologist for three years before she revealed her contamination thoughts and cleaning behaviors. Three years during which she lost four jobs because her cleaning behavior made her late for work frequently or she missed work entirely. When she did go to work thoughts of contamination and the cleaning behavior prevented her from completing tasks. Three years during which she missed her grandmother's funeral and her godsister's wedding because of the obsessive-compulsive behavior. Three years of hiding and concealing the truth from family, coworkers, and friends. Three years of suffering because, as she later revealed in a session, "I have a cousin who hears voices, and I didn't want folks to think I was crazy, too."

Rachel's lies ended one Sunday morning when she heard me on a radio program talking about OCD. She called in and began by saying, "I think I have what you're talking about." Then she went on to describe her life over the past three years. I encouraged her to tell her dermatologist about the hand washing. He administered the OCD screening test, and together they contacted me.

OCD OR NORMAL BEHAVIOR?

After reading this far, some of you may be wondering if your shopping, saving, checking, and praying behavior is possibly OCD. Let's face it, as Black women most of us have more than enough pairs of black shoes in our closet, have been trained from toddlerhood to keep a clean house, and spirituality is a major part of our lives.

If your mother-in-law—who raised your husband by herself, worked two jobs, and kept an immaculate house—is coming to visit and you spend three days cleaning because you don't want to hear her say you're not treating her son right, that's not

OCD. If there has been a burglary in the neighborhood and you check the doors and windows two or three times before you leave the house, that's not OCD. If your closet is full of clothes that you've worn only once, that's not OCD.

If all these things are not OCD, then what is? Dr. Wayne K. Goodman, chairman of the Department of Psychiatry at the University of Florida, has put together a very useful OCD screening tool that helps determine whether your repetitive behaviors and thoughts are excessive. Once this is determined, you can decide whether you should seek a professional assessment of your thoughts and behaviors. If you like, you can take the screening test (in its current version) right now.

A SCREENING TEST FOR OBSESSIVE-COMPULSIVE DISORDER

Women who have Obsessive-Compulsive Disorder (OCD) experience recurrent unpleasant thoughts and feel driven to perform certain acts over and over again. Although women usually recognize that the obsessions and compulsions are senseless or excessive, the symptoms of OCD often prove difficult to control without proper treatment. Obsessions and compulsions are not pleasurable; on the contrary, they are a source of distress. The following questions are designed to help you determine if you have symptoms of OCD.

PART A: Please Circle Yes or No

Over the past 30 days, have you been bothered by unpleasant thoughts or images that repeatedly enter your mind, such as:

1. concerns with contamination (dirt, germs,   YES   NO
   chemicals, radiation) or acquiring a serious
   illness such as AIDS?

2. overconcern with keeping objects (clothing,   YES   NO
   groceries, tools) in perfect order or arranged
   exactly?

3. images of death or other horrible events?   YES   NO

4. personally unacceptable religious or sexual   YES   NO
   thoughts?

*Over the past 30 days have you worried a lot about terrible things
happening, such as:*

5. fire, burglary, or flooding of the house?   YES   NO

6. accidentally hitting a pedestrian with your   YES   NO
   car or letting it roll down a hill?

7. spreading an illness (giving someone AIDS)?   YES   NO

8. losing something valuable?   YES   NO

9. harm coming to a loved one because you   YES   NO
   weren't careful?

*Over the past 30 days, have you worried about acting on an
unwanted and senseless urge or impulse, such as:*

10. physically harming a loved one, pushing a   YES   NO
    stranger in front of a bus, steering your car
    into oncoming traffic, inappropriate sexual
    contact, or poisoning dinner guests?

*Over the past 30 days, have you felt driven to perform certain acts
over and over again, such as:*

11. excessive or ritualized washing, cleaning, or   YES   NO
    grooming?

12. checking light switches, water faucets, the   YES   NO
    stove, door locks, or emergency brakes?

13. counting, arranging, or evening up behaviors such as making sure your socks are at the same height?   YES   NO

14. collecting useless objects or inspecting the garbage before it is thrown out?   YES   NO

15. repeating routine actions (such as getting in and out of a chair, going through a doorway, relighting a cigarette) a certain number of times until it feels *just right?*   YES   NO

16. feeling the need to touch other objects or people?   YES   NO

17. unnecessarily rereading or rewriting, or reopening envelopes before they are mailed?   YES   NO

18. examining your body for signs of illness?   YES   NO

19. avoiding colors (such as red because you think it symbolizes blood), numbers (such as 13 because you think it symbolizes bad luck), or names (such as those that begin with D because you believe it signifies death) that are associated with dreaded events or unpleasant thoughts?   YES   NO

20. feeling the need to "confess" or repeatedly ask for reassurance that you said or did something correctly?   YES   NO

PART B. The following questions refer to the repeated thoughts, images, urges, or behaviors you answered yes to in Part A. Make sure you circle the most appropriate number from 0 to 4.

1. On average, how much time is occupied by these thoughts or behaviors each day?

0	1	2	3	4
None	Mild (Less than 1 hr)	Moderate (1–3 hrs)	Severe (3–8 hrs)	Extreme (More than 8 hrs)

2. How much distress do these thoughts or behaviors cause you?

0	1	2	3	4
None	Mild	Moderate	Severe	Extreme

3. How hard is it for you to control these thoughts or behaviors?

0	1	2	3	4
Complete control	Much control	Moderate control	Little control	No control

4. How much do these thoughts and behaviors cause you to avoid doing anything or going anyplace or being with anyone?

0	1	2	3	4
No advoidance	Occasional advoidance	Moderate advoidance	Frequent and extensive	Extreme (housebound)

5. How much do they interfere with school, work, or your social or family life?

0	1	2	3	4
None	Slight interference	Definitely intereferes with functioning	Much interference	Extreme (disabling)

Sum on Part B (Add up score on questions 1–5)_____

Your Score and What It Means

As the questions you just answered illustrate, OCD is not about whether we engage in certain behaviors, but about the combination of thoughts and behaviors. If you answered yes to two or more questions in Part A and obtained a score of 5 or more in Part B, you may be experiencing OCD. Remember, however, that the questions you answered are just a screening test. To determine if you have OCD, you must undergo a thorough assessment by a mental health professional.

A THOROUGH ASSESSMENT

Rachel answered yes to questions 1 and 11 in Part A and received a score of 12 in Part B of the screening test. Based on her score, she and her dermatologist contacted me and requested a thorough assessment.

A thorough assessment is the psychological equivalent of a complete physical examination. In Rachel's case, the major question I wanted to answer was, Does she have OCD? But I needed to answer other questions as well. Is she experiencing any other form of anxiety? Is depression an issue? What is the overall state of her emotional health?

A complete assessment takes between two and two and half hours. Rachel's assessment took two hours and ten minutes. During the assessment, I conducted an in-depth interview, had Rachel complete several surveys and, as we talked, periodically assessed whether she was experiencing any obsessions or the strong urge to engage in compulsive behavior.

The assessment information indicated that Rachel did have OCD and that she was mildly depressed. Based on everything learned from the assessment, the dermatologist and I worked together to help Rachel manage her OCD. Part of the process involved professional therapy for the OCD and the depression. Today, Rachel's repetitive thoughts and behaviors are significantly reduced and she is leading a happy and productive life.

Notice that I did not say Rachel's OCD was cured. That's because there is no pill or therapy that will make the repetitive thoughts and behaviors go away forever. But Rachel has learned how to control and manage her OCD. She goes months without a repetitive thought or behavior. Every now and again, the obsessions and compulsions return. This is called "relapse." When a relapse occurs, rather than becoming upset and disappointed, Rachel uses the techniques and strategies she learned in therapy, the support of her Soothe Your Nerves Sister Circle, and books from her personal library to master her OCD. As a result, the relapse periods are extremely short and do not significantly disrupt her life. I'll talk more about OCD treatment in Chapters 8 and 9. However, it is important to remember that Rachel or any other Black woman will not be able to manage her OCD if she has not decided to let go of her secret. It is the secrecy that keeps Black women repeating their compulsions over and over again.

11 | SOOTHING NERVES

SIX

M.D., Ph.D., M.S.W.: What Therapist Is Right for Me?

*L*ate one evening as I sat in my office revising this manu-
script, the following e-mail message arrived.

> Help!!! Panic. I can't eat or sleep, and I've missed so
> much work that I'm in danger of losing my job. Please tell
> me you know someone in Chicago who can help me.
> Thanks for listening.
>
> BETTY B.

Every week I receive at least one e-mail similar to Betty's
from a woman whose life has been overtaken by anxiety. The
request is always the same: Please help me find someone in my
area who understands what is happening and can make it stop.
When I respond to these messages, I always ask what qualities
the person is looking for in a therapist. Most indicate they want
someone who knows what it is like to experience prejudice and
discrimination on the job, in the school, or in the department

store. Someone who understands what they mean when they say "I'm the only one" or "I'm one of a handful." Someone who comprehends what it is like to feel that you are too dark or too light, or your hair is too nappy, too straight, or too bad, and how these feelings contribute to anxiety and thoughts of never being able to measure up. Someone who understands how and why it is so difficult for Black women to admit they are anxious. These women are looking for a Black therapist.

The most expedient way to find a Black therapist is to call the national office of the Association of Black Psychologists, the Association of Black Psychiatrists, or the National Association of Black Social Workers. Contact information is listed in the Resources section at the end of this book. If you are unable to reach any of these organizations, the state licensing boards for each of these professions can provide the needed information. Several national anxiety organizations, such as the Anxiety Disorders Association of America, the Obsessive Compulsive Foundation, and Freedom from Fear, may also be able to help. These groups keep a nationwide list of anxiety professionals and may have information about a Black anxiety specialist in your area. When you call a national office, licensing board, or organization, make sure you specify that you are looking for someone who uses cognitive behavior therapy (CBT). Other types of therapy, such as psychoanalysis, are not as effective in overcoming anxiety.

TYPES OF THERAPISTS

Psychologists

The association you decide to call should be determined by the qualifications you are looking for in a therapist. If you want a doctor, you want either a psychologist or a psychiatrist. Most psychologists who are therapists have a Ph.D. or Psy.D. in clinical or counseling psychology and are licensed to practice in their state. At a minimum, psychologists have three years of rigorous academic training and a one-year internship, but they do not have a medical degree.

Psychiatrists

Psychiatrists are physicians, medical doctors. They have either an M.D. (doctor of medicine) or a D.O. (doctor of osteopathy). Psychiatrists have completed medical school, an internship, and a residency. They have a medical license and are board certified to practice psychiatry. In addition to conducting therapy, psychiatrists may also prescribe medication; the ability to prescribe medication is the major difference between a psychologist and a psychiatrist. You will often find psychologists and psychiatrists working together in a private practice, hospital, medical school, university clinic, or community mental health center.

Social Workers

Social workers have a master's degree and are also licensed to practice therapy. A master's degree consists of two years of academic and practical training. To be licensed as a social worker, an individual must have an additional two years of practical experience after obtaining the master's. Many health maintenance organizations (HMOs) and employee assistance programs (EAPs) use social workers as therapists.

Psychotherapists and Counselors

I would be remiss if I didn't say a word about a broad category of therapists known as psychotherapists or counselors. Over the years I have learned that training for this category of therapists varies widely. Many psychotherapists and counselors are well trained. The musical director for the Soothe Your Nerves workshops is a licensed professional clinical counselor; she has a master's degree and has completed a counseling internship. She has trained with several psychologists, including me, and I feel confident she is well trained.

Sadly, equal numbers of psychotherapists and counselors are not. I recently was consulted on a case involving a woman who suffered panic attacks and was seen by a psychotherapist who claimed to be licensed. He was—as a certified public accountant! This gentleman had neither the education nor the client training to practice anything but doing taxes.

Before you choose to work with a psychotherapist or counselor, make sure you ask about the person's training, whether he or she is licensed, and in what field. In choosing a psychotherapist or counselor you want someone who has at least a master's degree, has completed an internship, and is licensed to practice *therapy* in your state.

CHARLATANS AND SHYSTERS

Because anxiety can be so debilitating and many Black women are so desperate to get better, some so-called professionals offer instant cures. While some very good intensive programs do exist that can significantly reduce your anxiety in a week or two weeks, beware of anyone who says your anxiety can be cured in less than twenty-four or, for that matter, forty-eight hours.

Prior to contacting me, Tee contacted a man who claimed to be a Yoruba priest. He instructed Tee to go out and buy candles, matches, dragon's blood, and the eggs of a red hen from his wife's store. Tee was so desperate to get better she did as he asked. The priest came to her home and performed what Tee believed was an ancient African anxiety-cleansing ritual. In fact it was a ritual the man had developed based on his other career as a hoodoo doctor. The ritual left her $500 poorer and more anxious than she had been before the ceremony.

FINDING A BLACK THERAPIST

Many Black women may want a Black therapist but live in an area where a Black therapist is unavailable. In the Surgeon General's report, *Mental Health, Culture, Race, and Ethnicity*, Dr. David Satcher advises us that only 2 percent of psychiatrists, 2 percent of psychologists, and 4 percent of social workers are Black. The simple fact is that the number of Black mental health professionals is very small, and you may not be able to find one. If this is the case, you want to seek out a therapist who has expertise in what is known as multicultural issues. This means your therapist has the training and education to recognize and deal with issues that affect people of color. This is important because without multicultural training, your therapist may fail to understand what you are describing. Imagine telling your therapist that you are tired of being a strong Black woman, and she or he tells you to cease weightlifting. It's happened! The good news is many more therapists are trained in multicultural issues and are becoming easier to find. All you need to do is call the state licensing board, one of the national anxiety organizations discussed earlier, or the local physician's referral, and request the name of therapists in your area who specialize in multicultural issues.

Interviewing a Therapist

Tee's experience highlights the importance of interviewing a therapist before you begin therapy. If a therapist gets an attitude when you ask if she minds answering a few questions, thank her for her time and leave. A compassionate, caring competent therapist expects and encourages potential clients to ask questions.

What kind of questions should you ask? Ask her about her credentials. Make sure you understand whether she is a psychologist, psychiatrist, social worker, or counselor and what that means in terms of the services she can supply. Once in a while I receive a call from a woman who wants to see me about obtaining medication. This person has confused my role as a psychologist with that of a psychiatrist.

Ask the therapist about her experience in treating women with your anxiety difficulty. How many clients has she treated? Has treatment been successful? Ask her about the type of treatment she uses and ask her to explain it. If the therapist is of a different ethnic background, don't forget to ask about multicultural training. Finally, always, always ask a potential therapist about her license.

PAYING FOR THERAPY

After I answered Betty's e-mail, she wrote back:

> Dr. Barnett: Thank you for your words of encourage-
> ment and hope. I need to be honest. Given my job situa-
> tion, I don't have much money, and my insurance doesn't
> cover mental health. Is this therapist going to cost a lot?
>
> BETTY B.

Betty's predicament is similar to that of a significant number of Black women. Depending on your therapist's education, the cost of therapy may range from $75 to $175 per hour. Many insurance companies will pay a significant portion of the cost of cognitive behavior therapy, but women who work part-time or have to pay out of pocket for their insurance often do not have mental health coverage.

If you want professional help to overcome your anxiety, lack of insurance or inadequate insurance is not an obstacle. Insurance-free options exist. Many workplaces have an employee assistance program, more commonly known as EAP. Generally staffed by well-trained counselors and social workers, an EAP offers help at little or no cost. Your EAP counselor may refer you to a counselor outside of the workplace. In these cases your employer may or may not foot the bill.

Community mental health centers are another option. Most have a sliding scale fee, which means the cost is tailored to your income. Having spent two years as a therapist at a community mental health center in Chicago, I know firsthand that these mental health professionals are dedicated to their professions and their clients. Sometimes, given the number of people they see, community mental health center therapists don't have time to read the latest research or bestseller; that makes the collaborative nature of CBT very important. When you go for your first appointment at your local community mental health center, take along your copy of *Soothe Your Nerves* to share with your assigned therapist.

Another option that many Black women tend not to be aware of is university and medical school clinics. Many universities have clinics that serve both campus and community clients, with sliding scale fees available to community clients. A second campus option is the research clinics available at larger universities and those with medical schools. The bulk of what we know about the effective treatment of anxiety difficulties comes from data collected at the research and treatment clinics of universities and medical schools. Most of the information I am sharing with you in this book about anxiety and Black women comes from willingness of Black women to participate in my research studies.

I know, I know, research has a horrible reputation in Black communities because of the Tuskegee study and the prison behavior modification studies; however, much has changed since those studies were conducted. All universities and medical schools now have what is known as an institutional review board (IRB). Before anyone can conduct a study, it must be reviewed and approved by the IRB. For studies that involve treatment of any psychological or medical difficulty, the person in charge of the study must appear before the IRB and answer any questions board members have. This is done so the Tuskegee study and prison behavior modification studies never happen again.

Receiving therapy as part of a research study is safe and effective. In many cases you are receiving state-of-the-art CBT, and at no cost. That's right: Because the purpose of these clinics is to enhance existing CBT treatments, you are not charged for treatment. You will be asked to complete surveys and questionnaires about your anxiety and treatment. The researchers may ask your permission to monitor your heart rate and blood pressure as you complete tasks or undergo a specific experience. They may also ask for your feedback on how well you think they are conducting the study. I want to emphasize that throughout any research study you will always be *asked* to do things. You always have the right to say no.

Through our e-mail correspondence I discovered Betty was a twenty-minute El train ride away from a large university that had an anxiety research and treatment center. A faculty member was conducting a study on the treatment of panic disorder. Betty contacted the center's director and became enrolled in the panic study. She was able to receive CBT at no cost. In fact, the center gave her tokens for her train fare.

There are competent, compassionate, caring anxiety specialists throughout this country who understand the needs of Black women. Help is only a phone call or e-mail away.

❖

SEVEN

Nerve Pills

G IRL, I'M NOT TAKING no drugs." These were the first
words out of Callie's mouth when I arrived for our lunch.
"It's great to see you, too," I replied. "Now what's this about
drugs?" Callie smiled. "I'm sorry, Ang," she said. "I went to the
anxiety clinic you recommended, and after I met with the therapist, she scheduled an appointment for me with one of the psychiatrists in the practice. I'm telling you now, I'm not taking any
nerve pills."

When it comes to medication to soothe bad nerves, Black
women tend to fall into two camps: those like Callie who don't
want to rely on artificial means to deal with their anxiety, and
those who want medication because they believe it will cure
their anxiety. The choice to use or not use medication is up to
you and your doctor. Before making that decision, however, it is
important that you understand what medication will and will
not do. Medication alone won't cure you. No pill exists that
will completely eliminate anxiety, but medications exist that will
lower your anxiety to a manageable level. Whether you choose

prescription drugs or herbal remedies, medication takes the edge off one's anxiety. Your anxiety is reduced to a level that allows therapy or self-help to be beneficial. Medication prepares you for the process of overcoming anxiety.

Back in the day, if a Black woman was anxious, she went to her family doctor, and he prescribed something to calm her nerves. Nerve pills, Black folks called them, and believed they would feel better if they took them. The pills worked, but only for a little while, and many women became addicted to them.

The type of medication used to treat anxiety today is dramatically different from what was available years ago. Working together, psychologists, psychiatrists, and pharmaceutical companies have come up with new medications to treat various forms of anxiety. The effectiveness of these medications has increased, and the addictive properties and other side effects have decreased.

MEDICATIONS FOR ANXIETY

The most commonly prescribed medications for relieving anxiety symptoms fall into six general classifications: selective serotonin reuptake inhibitors, benzodiazepines, tricyclic antidepressants, beta-blockers, azaspirones, and monoamine oxidase inhibitors. Let's take a look at each classification.

Selective Serotonin Reuptake Inhibitors (SSRIs)

SSRIs are the newest class of drugs developed to relieve anxiety symptoms. They work by increasing the amount of serotonin, a hormone and neurotransmitter that exists between nerve endings in your brain. Five SSRIs are currently available.

I've listed their generic name first, followed by their brand name.

Fluvoxamine (Luvox)
Fluoxetine (Prozac)
Sertraline (Zoloft)
Paroxetine (Paxil)
Citalopram (Celexa)

You may have seen television ads for paroxetine (Paxil). These ads stress paroxetine's effectiveness in reducing generalized and social anxiety symptoms. It is also effective in diminishing panic attack symptoms, as is citalopram. Fluvoxamine and fluoxetine are quite helpful in reducing the obsessive thoughts associated with OCD.

All medications have possible side effects. Compared to other antianxiety medications, the side effects of SSRIs are relatively mild. The most common include headaches, weakness, sleep disturbances, dizziness, and tremors; in addition, a person may experience nausea, dry mouth, decreased sex drive, and weight gain.

Benzodiazepines

Benzodiazepines, the oldest legal form of antianxiety medications, are sedatives. This means they have a calming effect on the body. For this reason most medical doctors prescribe benzodiazepines to alleviate panic attack symptoms and the anticipatory anxiety associated with them. The three most commonly prescribed are alprazolam (Xanax), clonazepam (Klonopin), and lorazepam (Ativan).

Twenty-five years ago these were the drugs that Black folks were referring to when they used the term "nerve pills." The use of benzodiazepines has generated controversy among Black women. Some women like the benzodiazepines because it is possible to take them only when needed. Other women feel that the take-as-needed approach fosters a dependence on the medication. Rather than learning to master your panic, you learn to let the medication do all the work.

The truth is that benzodiazepines are helpful in reducing the intensity and number of panic attacks. The problem is that once you stop taking them, the panic attacks return, with more frequency and intensity. Psychiatrists call this a rebound effect. Thankfully, this effect is short-lived.

A second drawback to benzodiazepines is that they have addictive properties. Alprazolam, clonazepam, and lorazepam are newer benzodiazepines and less habit forming than the older ones. These days it is extremely rare for a Black woman with panic attacks to become addicted to a benzodiazepine. The risk of addiction increases dramatically, however, if alcohol is used as well as a benzodiazepine to control panic. Alcohol and benzodiazepines are an extremely dangerous combination. Anyone who uses alcohol to control anxiety symptoms should inform her doctor. This doesn't mean the doctor won't prescribe medication; it simply means she won't prescribe a benzodiazepine. The risk of addiction is simply too great.

The most common side effect of benzodiazepines is mild drowsiness. For older adults there may also be some weakness and confusion. Other possible side effects include lack of energy, slurred speech, dizziness, low blood pressure, incontinence, and interference with the menstrual cycle.

Tricyclic Antidepressants (TCAs)

Although generally used to treat depression, certain TCAs are effective in reducing anxiety symptoms. TCAs block the passage of natural neurochemical stimulants to the nerve endings of the brain, producing a calming effect. Two TCAs tend to be prescribed most frequently: clomipramine (Anafranil) is prescribed to reduce the obsessive thoughts associated with OCD, and imipramine (Tofranil) is prescribed to reduce panic attacks.

As you may recall, many anxious Black women also develop mild to moderate levels of depression. A secondary benefit of prescribing a TCA is that it helps reduce the level of depression experienced.

The most common side effects of TCAs include sedation, blurred vision, disorientation, confusion, hallucinations, dry mouth, tremors or spasms, urination difficulties, and sensitivity to bright light. Other possible side effects include changes in blood pressure, blood sugar level, and heart rate, nausea, loss of appetite, diarrhea, and changes in one's sex drive.

Beta-blockers

If you are a woman with hypertension, you may already be familiar with beta-blockers because they are primarily used to control high blood pressure. Psychiatrists have found that two of the beta-blockers, atenolol (Tenormin) and propranolol (Inderal), help reduce social anxiety that is limited to one or two situations. Atenolol and propranolol reduce anxiety by lowering the heart rate and blood pressure, thereby reducing symptoms such as sweating, rapid heartbeat, and going from cold to hot or hot to cold.

As you learned in Chapter 5, in the limited version of social anxiety, your symptoms are confined to one or two social situations, such as giving a talk or performing in front of others. Many women take beta-blocker medication only when they know they will be in a specific anxiety-provoking social situation. As with taking benzodiazepines, this take-as-needed scenario is viewed negatively by some women who do not want to become overly dependent on medication.

The ability of beta-blockers to reduce the symptoms of the limited version of social anxiety can be altered by combining them with other prescription or over-the-counter medications; for example, aspirin and products that contain aspirin can reduce the antianxiety benefits of atenolol and propranolol. The same holds true for estrogen. If your physician wants to prescribe a beta-blocker, make sure you give her a list of all prescription and nonprescription drugs you routinely take.

Women experience relatively few side effects from beta-blockers. In rare cases they may experience sleepiness, tiredness, cold feet and hands, disorientation, and depression. Occasionally, women will find that a beta-blocker increases their anxiety rather than reducing it.

Azaspirones

Currently, buspirone (Buspar) is the only medication that falls under this category. Buspirone works fairly quickly to reduce symptoms associated with generalized anxiety. While we know what mechanisms inside the body and brain are affected by the other antianxiety medications, we are still unclear about exactly how azaspirones work inside our body. What we do know is that for many women buspirone appears to be a safe and effective medication for generalized anxiety symptoms.

Some individuals who take the drug report drowsiness, while others report excitement. Other common side effects include headache, light-headedness, nervousness, heart palpitations, tremors, and sweating. On occasion buspirone has caused strokes, heart attacks, and heart failure in some patients.

Monoamine Oxidase Inhibitors (MAO Inhibitors)

MAO inhibitors are prescribed for women whose anxiety symptoms have not been reduced by SSRIs, benzodiazepines, beta-blockers, azaspirones, or TCAs. They work by breaking down certain hormones in the brain. The two MAO inhibitors prescribed for anxiety are phenelzine (Nardil) and tranyl-cypromine sulfate (Parnate).

The major drawback to MAO inhibitors is that you cannot eat or drink certain foods and beverages such as cheese, cured and processed meats, chocolate, or caffeine when taking them. These foods contain an ingredient called tyramine which, when combined with an MAO inhibitor, produces an adverse reaction.

Common side effects include dizziness, especially when rising from a sitting or reclining position, fainting, headaches, manic reactions, twitching, uncontrollable muscle movement, loss of appetite, weight changes, nausea, diarrhea, stomach pains, dry mouth, agitation, and sexual difficulties. Some women experience an increase rather than a decrease in anxiety symptoms.

MEDICATION CONSULTATION

Medication should always be prescribed by a medical doctor. Any physician can prescribe antianxiety medications. Psychiatrists, however, are medical doctors who are specifically trained to prescribe medication for anxiety and other emotional difficulties. Because of this training, I recommend that if you want medication to help alleviate your anxiety symptoms, you should schedule an appointment with a psychiatrist. During your appointment the psychiatrist will take a medical history and conduct a thorough assessment of your symptoms. She will ask you questions about your anxiety, your mood, your thoughts, and your health as well as monitor your blood pressure and your heart rate. Only when the assessment is complete will she prescribe medication. In all likelihood you will be prescribed a small dose, and your psychiatrist will monitor your symptoms and the amount of medication in your bloodstream on a weekly or biweekly basis. The amount of medication will be gradually increased or decreased depending on your body's response. Your psychiatrist will also inform you of all possible side effects, not just the common ones, and will want to know immediately if you begin to experience any of them.

If your family physician prescribes antianxiety medication, you must learn to advocate on your own behalf. Be sure to give her an accurate description of your symptoms. Many women find it helpful to write down the physical and emotional feelings they experience and bring the list with them to the doctor's appointment. Ask your doctor how often she will schedule appointments to monitor the effectiveness of the medication. Together you and the doctor should develop a plan of action as to what to do if you begin experiencing side effects. Inquire whether she wants you to come in, phone the office, or stop taking the medication.

A week after our lunch, Callie met with the psychiatrist and voiced her concerns about medication. The psychiatrist listened very carefully and patiently addressed each of her concerns. Satisfied with the answers she received, Callie agreed to use medication to "take the edge off" her anxiety. The psychiatrist prescribed a small dose of imipramine. The combination of medication and therapy worked fairly quickly. Within three months the psychiatrist began tapering the dosage, and by six months Callie was medication free. More important, her anxiety symptoms were almost nonexistent.

SHARING PILLS AND HALVING PILLS

In the movie *Kingdom Come*, the Slocumb family gathers for the funeral of the family patriarch, Woodrow "Bud" Slocumb. In one scene Charisse, played by Jada Pinkett Smith, asks Lucille, portrayed by Viveca A. Fox, if she can borrow a nerve pill. It seems Charisse has left her nerve pills at home and needs one badly. Lucille goes into the bathroom, downs a nerve pill herself, then brings out two for Charisse. "Here, Charisse honey," she says. "I brought you a double dose."

Sharing nerve pills as Lucille and Charisse do in *Kingdom Come* is a common practice among anxious Black women. Usually the shared pill is a benzodiazepine. We share nerve pills because we mistakenly believe that like over-the-counter medication, they'll work for anybody. The medication your doctor prescribes is based on your symptoms and your body chemistry. Chances are the pills will be too weak or too strong for the other person.

My client Jalesa learned this lesson the hard way. Ever since she was a little girl, she and her mother had always clashed. Last summer, her mother came to visit and, true to form, the visit was stressful and anxiety provoking. As Jalesa recalled it,

"One evening my mother got on my nerves so bad, I gave her one of my pills. She took it, but she was also taking medication for her heart. She had a reaction, and I had to rush her to the hospital." "Dr. Barnett," Jalesa wailed, "I almost killed my mama."

Jalesa's mother survived, and the incident led them to begin working on repairing their relationship. Today Jalesa and her mother laugh about what happened, but their story serves as a reminder that nerve pills are not mints. You cannot offer one to a friend or your mother just because you know she needs one.

On a related subject, let's talk about halving pills. Some medication is very expensive even when insurance picks up the bulk of the cost. And what if we don't have prescription coverage or any insurance at all? Sometimes in an effort to conserve our money and our medication, we cut pills in half. We figure half a pill is half a dose, and the anxiety symptoms will be only half as bad. Unfortunately, when it comes to medication, long division doesn't apply. Never physically cut your medication in half unless your doctor tells you to.

If you cannot afford the cost of the prescription, don't despair. Many pharmaceutical companies have programs that provide free medication to individuals who cannot afford it. Some paperwork is required, and your doctor must make the request. The Pharmaceutical Research and Manufacturers of America publishes a directory for physicians that lists all the programs available for those who cannot pay for their medications. If your doctor is unaware of this free directory, please tell her that it exists and that she can order it by calling 1-800-762-4636; it can also be downloaded from the organization's website at www.phrma.org.

NATURE'S REMEDIES

Many of us grew up with mothers, aunts, or grandmothers who were knowledgeable in herbal remedies: garlic in the winter to prevent colds, ginger tea during your period to reduce cramps, yams to reduce the number of sickle-cell crises. These women knew the importance of natural sources of healing. Today many psychological and medical experts are affirming the power of herbs and other natural remedies in reducing anxiety.

Ginseng and Chamomile

In their book, *Natural Health for African Americans,* Drs. Marcellus A. Walker and Kenneth B. Singleton speak of the power of natural healing in dealing with anxiety. Recognizing the role of stress in producing anxiety, Drs. Walker and Singleton highlight the short-term stress-reducing properties of ginseng and chamomile.

Ginseng and chamomile are natural nervine relaxants; translated, these herbs help soothe frayed nerves. If stress plays a role in your anxiety, you may find that ginseng and chamomile in the form of tea, powder, pill, or bath provide short-term relief. You will notice a reduction in your stress level, which will produce a decrease in your level of anxiety.

I want to emphasize that ginseng and chamomile are only short-term solutions. The key is to combine them with other strategies such as therapy, self-help, or meditation to produce long-term effects in overcoming your anxiety.

Lavender

As little girls, my younger sister and I loved to sneak into my mother's bedroom and play with her creames, perfumes, and powders. My sister liked the smell of mommy's Pond's cold cream; I loved the smell of her lavender sachets and soaps. For years I considered lavender only a flower used to make perfume, and then one day I walked into an upscale supermarket and was offered a piece of lavender bread. It was then I learned that lavender was actually an herb and the flower part of the plant was used for much more than perfume. For centuries lavender has been used to prepare foods for those with "delicate constitutions" or "nervous conditions."

Lavender provides short-term relief for many of the symptoms associated with generalized anxiety. The dried flowers can be used to make a tea that helps reduce tension and stress headaches. The crushed flower can be mixed in foods to quell queasy or upset stomachs. Just smelling lavender can reduce your anxiety. Researchers at the Touch Research Institute at the University of Miami Medical School found that inhaling the scent of lavender essential oil for three minutes reduced anxiety, induced a feeling of relaxation, and elevated one's mood.

Similar to ginseng and chamomile, lavender offers only a partial, temporary solution to the reduction of generalized anxiety symptoms. Lavender can be combined with relaxation and therapy to ease the symptoms of generalized anxiety.

Kava Kava

Kava kava is a natural herb that is effective in alleviating the symptoms of mild to moderate panic attacks and generalized anxiety. A member of the pepper tree family, kava kava grows in the South Pacific Islands region that includes Samoa, Fiji, Tahiti, Tonga, and Papua New Guinea. Pacific Islanders have known about the anxiety-reducing properties of kava kava for hundreds of years. A beverage made from the root is used to induce tranquility and is drunk at the end of the workday. In some South Pacific cultures, before people come together to resolve a dispute a kava kava beverage is sipped because, as western traveler Tom Harrisson wrote in 1937, "You cannot hate with kava in you."

Nonetheless, it wasn't until the late twentieth century that most Westerners became aware of the benefits of kava kava. Amazed by the herb's power to calm, several European psychiatrists conducted studies on kava kava's effectiveness in reducing anxiety. They found that taken in powdered capsule form, it effectively reduces anxiety symptoms. Doctors have found, however, that when one uses kava kava capsules longer than three months, a risk of addiction develops. I must point out that the capsule form is far less potent than the drink. In beverage form, kava kava can produce an intoxicated-like state. Similar to alcohol, kava kava should not be taken if you are also taking a benzodiazepine.

In March 2002 the Food and Drug Administration (FDA) issued a warning that kava kava may be linked to liver damage. This warning came on the heels of similar warnings being issued in Europe and Canada. Although the actual number of reported cases is rare, the damage to the liver is so severe that the FDA felt kava kava users should be warned. Before taking kava kava it is important to consult your psychiatrist or family physician about the risks and benefits. If a history of liver disease runs in your family or you already take medications that can affect the liver, kava kava may not be the herb for you.

Valerian

One of the most popular herbs on the market, valerian is used primarily as a sleep aid. Made from the part of the plant that grows underground, valerian is a sedative, and many women swear by its ability to give you a good night's sleep without feeling groggy in the morning.

For over two centuries valerian has also been used to soothe bad nerves. Women with generalized anxiety find it helpful in reducing the restlessness and insomnia associated with this form of anxiety. Others have found it useful for mild levels of anxiety that arise in stressful situations. To the best of my knowledge, no scientific studies have been conducted to test valerian's effectiveness on various forms of anxiety. Experiments have been conducted that show valerian helps promote sleep in women whose anxiety keeps them awake at night. As an added bonus, these women also experience a decrease in their daytime anxiety.

Valerian is a sedative, and if you are sensitive to prescription or over-the-counter sedatives, you are likely to be sensitive or allergic to valerian. Valerian promotes sleep, so if you decide to try it, after consulting with your psychiatrist or family physician, be careful when and where you take it and how much you take. Many experts recommend that valerian be used for no longer than six weeks. The biggest drawback to using valerian is the smell. Scientists and consumers alike have described it as a cross between dirty gym socks and moldy cheese.

Herbs do not cure anxiety. Like kava kava, valerian reduces the anxiety, but you must engage in other work to completely overcome the anxiety difficulties in your life.

SELF-MEDICATION

For some Black women the anxiety and fear experienced is so debilitating they are willing to take anything to make it go away. These women use alcohol and other substances in an attempt to get rid of the anxiety. This is known as self-medication.

Several of the women you've met in this book—Glenda, Janise, Clarice and Callie—engaged in a form of self-medication. For Glenda and Janise it was alcohol, for Clarice it was crack, and for Callie it was food, especially anything with chocolate. As you know from their stories, self-medication seldom works.

At the end of a hard day, many Black women use alcohol to unwind. At moderate levels over a short period of time, alcohol reduces anxiety, but anxious women, particularly those who experience panic attacks or social phobia, tend to use high amounts of alcohol over longer periods of time. The result is an increase in anxiety.

In the 1980s many professionals I knew who used drugs extolled the virtues of cocaine. It was the drug of choice because at the time people believed you couldn't become addicted to it. After an intense week of work and life pressures, "doing a line of coke" on the weekend was seen by some as a great way, albeit an expensive way, to unwind.

Today we know both of those assertions are false. Cocaine and its derivative, crack, are addictive. They are also stimulants and increase anxiety. You don't unwind with cocaine or crack, you become more tightly wound, although in the midst of a cocaine rush or a crack high, you may not realize it.

Caffeine is also a stimulant and increases anxiety. Yes, caffeine, the stuff that is found in coffees, teas, colas, and chocolate.

Caffeine is one of the first things we reach for when we are stressed, upset, or anxious. I, for one, would never have made it through my Ph.D. program without Häagen-Dazs Chocolate Chocolate Chip Ice Cream. Caffeine is an anxious Black woman's worst enemy. It is cheap, legal, easy to purchase, found in foods and beverages that taste great, and a very, very difficult habit to break.

Self-medication, in whatever form, helps Black women hide their real problem from the world. It offers only fleeting benefits and in all cases makes the anxiety worse.

Medication alone will not cure anxiety. The most effective treatment for the various forms of anxiety is cognitive behavior therapy (CBT).

EIGHT

Cognitive Behavior Therapy

*E*ARLY ONE SATURDAY, as I sat reading my devotions, my business phone rang. I ignored it, thinking it was my older sister, because no one else I knew possessed the courage to call me at six o'clock in the morning. I was wrong. When the answering machine picked up, I heard an unfamiliar female voice say, "Hello, Dr. Barnett. My name is Sharon. I saw you on BET talking about CBT. I have panic attacks, and I've been taking nerve pills for two years, but I'm still not better. Can you tell me more about CBT?"

As you already have read, CBT stands for cognitive behavior therapy. My friend, the eminent anxiety specialist Dr. David Barlow, describes CBT as a process by which the cause and effect relationships between thoughts, feelings, and behaviors are evaluated. In addition, relatively straightforward strategies to lessen symptoms and reduce avoidant behavior are employed.

MISPERCEPTIONS ABOUT CBT

Some of you reading this chapter began scowling the moment you read the word "therapy." Although we are now more open about seeking professional help than we were in the past, therapy for Black women remains a sensitive subject. As with suicide, many of us believe therapy is something a Strong Black Woman doesn't do. Therapy is for women who cannot solve their own problems, women who are weak, not strong. To enter into therapy is to allow someone else to see our full range of emotions; in essence, it lets someone see us in our most vulnerable state.

Black women who choose CBT as an option for overcoming anxiety difficulties are not weak. On the contrary, it takes a Strong Black Woman to admit that she needs help with her anxiety. CBT can provide her with the assistance she needs to overcome anxiety problems.

Some in the Black community are wary of behavior therapy because they believe it is the same as behavior modification. Behavior modification involves receiving and surrendering credits for appropriate and inappropriate behavior. In the sixties behavior modification was used unethically in prisons to restrict freedom and limit choice. Cognitive behavior therapy is *not* behavior modification. Freedom of choice is essential to CBT. Cognitive behavior therapy is a participatory process in which you and the therapist work together to overcome your anxiety difficulty. Your therapist will not "make you do" anything you are unwilling to do or anything she is not willing to do herself.

Misperceptions about therapy in general, and cognitive behavior therapy in particular, keep us from seeking professional help for anxiety difficulties. Having cleared up the major misunderstandings, let's talk about what is involved in CBT.

COMPONENTS OF CBT

A major component of CBT is helping the anxious person understand the relationships between her thoughts, feelings, and behaviors. Many Black women struggling with anxiety feel helpless, out of control, and sorry for themselves. Others are angry they are in this predicament. Both groups fail to make the connection that it is their thoughts and feelings which in large part are keeping them anxious.

Self-Monitoring

To assist you in making the connection, the first thing many CBT therapists will teach you to do is self-monitor, a relatively simple CBT procedure. Individuals are simply asked to record their anxiety episodes for a weeklong period. A woman who experiences panic attacks would write down every time she has a panic attack; a woman with generalized anxiety would write down every time she worried; and a woman with OCD would record her obsessions and compulsions. When you self-monitor, you will want to record all the details; when and where you experienced the anxiety; what you were doing right before the anxiety occurred; what you did afterward; and what emotions you experienced before, during, and after the attack. Many therapists provide a paper or electronic journal to record these responses.

The following is a paper-and-pencil self-monitoring sheet adapted from my NIMH-funded study on panic attacks and hypertension.

SELF-MONITORING SHEET

ACTIVITY	POSTURE: sit/stand/recline LOCATION: home/work/other
Please circle your activity at the time of the panic attack (circle all that apply)	*Please circle the panic symptoms you experienced*
Going to sleep Resting Washing/dressing /grooming Urinating/defecating Driving/riding as a passenger Eating/drinking (non-alcohol) Housework Walking/shopping Sexual activity Other physical activity _____ Talking/listening Reading Typing/working on computer Watching TV/listening to radio Thinking Exercising Outdoor activities (gardening, mowing lawn) Childcare/eldercare/caregiving Other _____	Difficulty breathing Rapid heartbeat Choking/ smothering Sweating Trembling/shaking Nausea Fear of losing control Chest pain discomfort Hot/cold flashes Numbness/tingling Feeling unreal Lightheaded/dizzy Fear of dying

In the introduction to the self-monitoring journal, I remind women of the importance of recording their symptoms and activities as soon as possible after recognizing they were having a panic attack. Some women wanted to wait until the end of the day to fill out the journal. This defeats the purpose of self-monitoring. What you think you remember about an anxiety experience an hour or more after the fact is often very different from—and far worse than—what actually happened. By recording the event as soon as you recognize what is happening, you become more aware of how your negative thoughts and feelings are connected to your expression of anxiety.

Changing the Way You Think

The motivational speaker Les Brown tells us "we are what we think about most." In other words, what we think, we speak and we become. Anxious Black women who constantly engage in negative, self-defeating, and "what if" thinking begin to believe in their hearts, minds, and spirits that what they think is true and there is no hope. As a result, the anxiety and fear increase, and depression develops.

In CBT, women learn to change the way they think. An anxious Black woman becomes so accustomed to thinking a certain way that she does not realize it is negative. Thus, the first step for an anxious Black woman to change the way she thinks is recognizing that her thoughts are negative. The second step is learning to replace those negative, anxiety-producing thoughts with positive, affirming ones. Sounds simple enough, doesn't it? But it is not. When a Black woman is experiencing anxiety difficulties, it is much easier for her to think about herself in a negative way than in a positive one. Initially, seeing oneself in a positive light is hard work.

Try this simple test. Take a piece of paper and draw a line down the middle. On the left side write the word *strengths* and on the right side write the word *weaknesses*.

Strengths   Weaknesses

Underneath each heading make a list of your strengths and weaknesses. Which was easier to do? Most anxious Black women, and quite a few nonanxious ones, find that compiling a list of their weaknesses is easier than compiling a list of their strengths.

One of the first things said by Shauna, the college student whose cousin urged her to see me, when she walked into my office was "I can't go on like this." This statement conveyed negativity and hopelessness. Before she left my office that day, Shauna replaced that negative statement with the positive statement, "I'm just having panic attacks. They are treatable. I won't have to go on this way."

Changing the way you think about yourself and your anxiety takes time and practice. Whereas it may be easy to recognize a thought is negative, coming up with a positive one to replace it can be challenging. Many women become frustrated and think about giving up. Your frustration is just a temporary setback, and as the title of a recent book advises us, "A setback is just a setup for a comeback."

So What?

Negative self-statements are only one piece of the cognitive/mental component of anxiety. The other piece is the "what if" thoughts that figure so prominently in anxiety difficulties, especially for women with generalized anxiety and social phobia.

CBT helps women develop the skills to challenge and deconstruct the erroneous beliefs and catastrophic thoughts that are the hallmark of "what if" thinking by using what I and several other anxiety experts call "so what" thinking. "So what" thinking allows women to break free of the doubts perpetuated by "what if" thinking. It allows an individual to recognize that what she thinks is going to happen is far worse than what can actually happen. Maya, the law school assistant professor from my church, learned to do just that. One of the requirements for keeping her position was to publish law articles, but every time Maya sat down to write, she experienced a panic attack and her mind would fill with "what if"s. To counteract that, she engaged in a "so what" session with her therapist:

Therapist: So what if the article never gets published?

Maya: Well, I might lose my job.

Therapist: So what would happen if you lost your job?

Maya: I wouldn't have any money. My bills would pile up.

Therapist: So what would happen then?

Maya: I'd have to get a new job.

Therapist: So what? You wouldn't be able to get one?

Maya: Of course not. My law degree's from Harvard.

Therapist: So what?

Maya: So what? I have a Harvard law degree, the best law school in the country. I can get another job. Oh . . . I can get another job.

Therapist: So even if you write an article and it's horrible and the article never gets published and you lose your job, you could get another job?

Maya: Yes. I'd forgotten about all the options that are available to me. It's okay to send out my article, and if it gets rejected, well, so what?

ELIMINATING PHYSICAL SYMPTOMS
AND TENSION

The second major component of CBT centers on learning how to lessen the physical symptoms of anxiety difficulties without medication. This involves self-talk for all anxiety difficulties, breathing retraining for the panic attacks, and relaxation for the physical tension produced by the "what if" thoughts that are especially troublesome for women with generalized anxiety and social phobia.

Self-Talk

When Tee began to work with a cognitive behavior therapist, one of the first things she learned was self-talk. When a panic attack began, Tee would say softly to herself, "This is a panic attack. It will pass. The rapid heartbeat and breathing are just reactions. If I slow my breathing, the other symptoms will slow down, too. There is no reason to be afraid. It is just a panic attack. It will pass." Self-talk allowed Tee to take the panic out of the attack.

Self-talk is not limited to panic attacks. Women with OCD use it to remind themselves "It's not me, it's my OCD." Women with specific and social phobia use it to remind themselves that "it's just a fear, not a reality."

One concern many women have is that engaging in self-talk will make them look crazy. This is not true. Have you ever observed an athlete before an important play, an actress before she goes on stage, or a colleague before a meeting? Each one, in her own way, is practicing self-talk. As women become more adept at it, self-talk moves from soft to silent. But in the beginning, given the intensity of the anxiety-filled thoughts, self-talk is talk.

Breathing Retraining

Breathing retraining is a procedure specifically for women with unexpected panic attacks. Predicated on the role carbon dioxide plays in this form of anxiety, breathing retraining reduces the physical symptoms of panic attacks, promotes relaxation, and allows the person to distinguish between panic symptoms and those associated with overbreathing. As children we learn that our nose is for breathing, yet many of us actually breathe through our mouths, expelling air from our lungs. For women with panic attacks, using the mouth to breathe can produce sensations similar to a panic attack. In breathing retraining, you first learn to pay attention to how you breathe. Then you learn to breathe at a natural rate (as opposed to a fast or slow one) using your diaphragm, mouth, and nose. Similar to the other components and techniques of CBT, breathing retraining requires practice. In the beginning, CBT therapists will recommend that you practice twice a day.

Ruth, the woman who suffered from hyperventilation episodes, believes that breathing retraining was crucial in helping her overcome panic attacks. "I was a chronic hyperventilator," she told me, "and the panic education course you recommended helped me make the connection between hyperventilation and panic. Once I learned to pay attention to my breathing, it cut in half the number of panic attacks and hyperventilation episodes. With breathing retraining and other CBT techniques, I have been panic free for nine months, and I haven't hyperventilated in ten months."

Progressive Muscle Relaxation

Relaxation and anxiety are incompatible. Various styles of relaxation exist; the most common include progressive muscle relaxation, deep muscle relaxation, deep breathing, and imagery. Anxiety experts agree, and numerous research studies have confirmed, that progressive muscle relaxation is the most powerful form of relaxation to use with an anxious woman. Progressive muscle relaxation was first developed by psychologist Edmund Jacobson. The body is divided into seven muscle groups, and individuals are taught how to tense and relax each group.

When I teach progressive relaxation, I lower the lights and have the client sit in a comfortable chair and remove her high-heel shoes. I begin by having the client take several cleansing breaths. Then I say, "Let's start with your hands and lower arms. I want you to make two fists, so tight that you can feel the tension. Make them tighter. And now relax. Feel the tension draining. Feel what it is like to have your hands and lower arms completely relaxed." After all muscles groups are tensed and relaxed, I ask the client to "take inventory of your entire body. Is there any area that still feels tense, any area that isn't relaxed? If so, let's go back and tense and relax that area."

Many CBT therapists tape the first progressive muscle relaxation session and give you a copy to take home so you will be able to practice. When I give a client a progressive muscle relaxation tape, I recommend that she practice twice a day. With practice, progressive muscle relaxation becomes automatic. At the first sign of physical tension, most clients are able to relax their entire bodies within thirty seconds.

Janise found progressive relaxation very helpful in dealing

with her fear of being accused of acting white. Before she entered predominantly Black social situations, she would completely relax her body. When she interacted with other African Americans, if she felt fear rising, she would tense all her muscles and relax. Over time, she felt more comfortable and confident in Black and mixed-race situations. She also gained self-assurance in the way she chose to define herself as a Black woman. When, at a party to celebrate the success of the college's basketball team, someone said she talked like a white girl. Janise replied, "Really. That's interesting. I think I talk like me."

ELIMINATING AVOIDANCE BEHAVIORS
Gradual Exposure and Systematic Desensitization

The third major component of CBT focuses on eliminating avoidance or agoraphobic behavior. One way this is accomplished is by using a hierarchical approach. Gradual exposure and systematic desensitization are two different forms of the hierarchical approach. In both forms, being in the situation you fear or facing the thing you are afraid of is broken into small steps that range from the least to the most anxiety provoking. This is known as a hierarchy. Together you and your therapist complete each step in the hierarchy. There are several ways this is accomplished. Your therapist may have you visualize yourself in the situation, use virtual reality, or have you actually engage in the task or interact in the situation. This third way is known as in vivo exposure. Exposure sessions generally last two hours. Whatever option you and your therapist decide on, the process is the same. When you begin the session, your anxiety builds, reaches its zenith, and then begins to dissipate. At first it may be difficult to stay in the situation, but with the support of your therapist and the use of the positive statements you develop as part of cognitive restructuring, you are able to do so.

As a Black woman you will find that after successfully completing each task, you gain a sense of mastery, and the anxiety and fear are diminished. Soon you are able with a minimum of discomfort to enter situations or perform tasks that formerly produced high anxiety.

Systematic desensitization differs from graduated exposure in that it is usually done by visualization or virtual reality, and the anxiety is paired with relaxation. The guiding principle behind systematic desensitization is that anxiety and relaxation are incompatible. If you are relaxed, you cannot be anxious. Systematic desensitization begins with your being in a relaxed state. Once you are completely relaxed, you visualize the lowest level situation on your hierarchy. As you begin to experience anxiety, you switch back to the relaxed state. Once you are relaxed again, you reenter the situation in your imagination. You continue in this fashion until the anxiety generated by the first item in the hierarchy has been desensitized. In other words, it no longer exists. The same procedure is repeated for successive levels of the hierarchy.

With gradual exposure and systematic desensitization the most important piece is the hierarchy. Great care must be taken to build it so that it reflects a steady progression from the lowest to the highest level of anxiety

Tee and her therapist chose to use gradual exposure to treat her agoraphobic behavior. Here is the hierarchy they put together:

TEE'S HIERARCHY

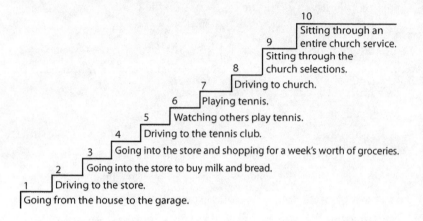

10 | Sitting through an entire church service.
9 | Sitting through the church selections.
8 | Driving to church.
7 | Playing tennis.
6 | Watching others play tennis.
5 | Driving to the tennis club.
4 | Going into the store and shopping for a week's worth of groceries.
3 | Going into the store to buy milk and bread.
2 | Driving to the store.
1 | Going from the house to the garage.

Tee and her therapist agreed to use an in vivo approach. "The hardest item for me was going back to church," Tee recalls. "My therapist was great. She helped me break the task into three parts: driving to church, listening to the choir selections, and staying for the entire church service. The second time we listened to the choir selections, I was enjoying myself so much that I wanted to stay. I forgot all about being afraid of having a panic attack and actually got an attitude with my therapist when we had to leave."

Gradual Exposure and Response Prevention

Gradual exposure is not just effective for avoidance behavior or agoraphobia. Paired with a CBT technique called response prevention, it is effective in helping reduce obsessive-compulsive symptoms. In this style of CBT the person is exposed to the situations that reflect the content of the obsessions and then is prevented from engaging in the compulsions.

Rachel, whose obsessions were concentrated in the area of germs and contamination, was placed in situations where she touched old banana peels, brushed her hair and teeth over the bathroom sink, and fixed lunch. After each activity she was forbidden to wash her hands or clean up the area she had just dirtied. Instead, we continued on with her normal routine for the day.

At first Rachel was beside herself. "What if I contaminated someone and they died?" she thought. "What if I myself was contaminated?" Her anxiety and the urge to clean and wash her hands were overwhelming. Just when she thought she couldn't stand the anxiety and obsessions one more second, they began to go away. The same thing happened in the next therapy session and the one after that. Soon, with repeated gradual exposure, response prevention, and practice, Rachel found that her obsessions and compulsions were almost nonexistent.

Flooding

Some CBT therapists don't use a hierarchical approach; they use a technique called flooding. In my workshops I tell people flooding is a lot like the way my Aunt Tibby learned to swim. Her cousins took her down to the river and threw her in. Aunt Tibby told me that when she hit that water, she was determined to fight her way back to shore and started splashing and thrashing, but that only made matters worse and she started to sink. Just as she was going under for the second time, she realized that if she stopped fighting and went with the flow of the river, she'd be okay.

Like Aunt Tibby and her swimming lesson, thousands of Black women are sinking in their own rivers of anxiety and fear. Flooding directly exposes you to the situation or thing you fear most. There are no gradual in-between steps. If you go with the flow, what you learn is that anxiety has its limits, and once it reaches a certain point, it naturally begins to dissipate. As you repeatedly expose yourself to flooding experiences, your anxiety level gets lower. In a matter of weeks you find yourself going places and doing things that you haven't been able to do in years.

Willa Mae chose the flooding approach. Yes, Willa Mae, my mother's dear friend with the cat phobia. During the time I was writing this book, she fell in love with a seventy-five-year-old man who owned a Winnebago and wanted to marry her. For their honeymoon he planned a three-month motor home tour to see all five of the Great Lakes. Willa Mae loved him, but being at campsites and near water meant there might be cats. She considered calling off the wedding. Then she saw an episode of *20/20* that featured phobias and flooding, and she asked my mother to ask me for a referral. After a thorough assessment, Willa Mae and her therapist entered a room where there was a live cat. In two flooding sessions her lifelong fear of cats was vanquished. She decided not to do anything about her fear of bridges. From now on her new husband would be doing all the driving.

Whether you and your CBT therapist choose to use a hierarchical approach or flooding, the hardest thing you will be asked to do is take the first step. For many women the thought of putting themselves in an anxiety-producing situation is so frightening, they have a panic attack. But as the ancient Chinese philosopher Lao-Tzu reminds us, "A journey of a thousand miles begins with the first step."

GROUP CBT

Although large numbers of women are treated individually, some CBT therapists may choose to treat several anxious women in the same session. Known as group therapy, it can be very effective. Group therapy provides the support of women who are experiencing similar anxiety difficulties and is particularly helpful for women with OCD.

After three months of individual therapy, Isabelle's therapists referred her to group therapy, and she found it very helpful for her OCD. Participating in exposure and response prevention with others seemed easier and less frightening than engaging in these techniques with her therapist alone. One group session consisted of a "slumber party" at a local hotel. The group members engaged in such behavior as messing up the room and leaving it that way, sharing popcorn from the same bowl, shouting out "sinful" thoughts, and going to bed without saying prayers, checking windows, or washing their hands. "At first it was hard," said Isabelle. "But as the night went on, I gained courage and inspiration from the other women, and they gained the same from me. The slumber party was a major step in my learning to manage my OCD."

Group therapy is not for everyone. For some women the anxiety is so overpowering and other emotional problems are so complex they need to work with a professional therapist on an individual basis. Individually or in groups, CBT works, and in dramatic ways, but for it to be effective, you must be willing to work with your therapist and practice what you learn outside of therapy.

After a recent Soothe Your Nerves workshop, an audience

member approached me and said she wanted to change therapists.

"Why?" I asked.

"My therapist makes me work," she said.

"Makes you work how?" I asked.

"She has me doing things I haven't done in years. In yesterday's session we walked to the corner drugstore, and I bought a pair of stockings."

"She walked with you?" I asked.

"Yes, but I had to do all the work. I had to tell her how I was feeling physically and the thoughts that were going through my mind. Now she's given me homework where I have to go to the drugstore by myself. That woman seems to forget I have bad nerves."

NINE

Faith, Hope, and Therapy

S EVERAL YEARS AGO I sat on the dais at a large church, waiting to talk about anxiety and Black women. The choir finished singing, and the minister rose to introduce me. "Dr. Barnett is a psychologist," he said. "Now I know all about psychologists. You all know I studied psychology in college. I know what psychologists do. If you just keep your mind on Jesus, you won't need a psychologist. Dr. Barnett, baby, come on up and say a few words."

Too often we as Black women are taught that faith and psychology are polar opposites. It is either faith or psychology; it can't be both. This belief is exemplified in an ad that recently ran in my local newspaper:

BIBLE-BASED COUNSELING. NO PSYCHOLOGY NEEDED.

It's not just our spiritual leaders. Psychologists and psychiatrists are just as guilty of perpetuating an either-or choice between psychology and faith. For many years faith was viewed as a crutch used by weak-minded people who refused to face the truth. People who relied on faith to help them were in denial. Black women who heard from God were suspected of hallucinating. Then psychologists and psychiatrists made a discovery: Faith helps people recover from emotional distress. In many cases it appears that people who actively practice their faith recover more rapidly than others. Faith engenders hope, and hope embodies a positive element that is crucial in overcoming emotional distress. More and more therapists are encouraging people to incorporate their faith-based practices into the anxiety recovery process.

As a little girl in Vacation Bible School, I learned that "faith is the substance of things hoped for, the evidence of things unseen." As an adult and psychologist this simple definition of faith remains at the core of any larger definitions of the term. In his book, *Stages of Faith: The Psychology of Human Development and the Quest for Meaning*, psychologist James Fowler defines faith as shared centers of values and power that join people to communities of shared trusts and loyalties. Faith, Fowler explains, gives form and content to our vision of the ultimate. In nonpsychological terms, Fowler is saying that no matter what your faith, it provides you with evidence of things unseen.

Historically, as Black women our faith has sustained us. The tools of our faith—prayer, meditation, affirmations, and music—can be put into action to change the anxious state of our minds and bodies, allowing us to break free of debilitating anxiety. It is a universal truth that if we can alter our minds, we can alter our lives. Combining our faith with CBT gives us the beliefs, words, and actions to do just that.

PRAYER

Whatever your faith, an essential component of it is prayer. Prayer takes many forms. There are prayers of thanksgiving, "Allah be praised for another panic-free day," and prayers of lament, "Dear God, I can't stand it. Do something now"; there are group prayers, solo prayers, directed prayers, scripted prayers, impromptu prayers—the list goes on. Theologian Richard J. Foster has delineated twenty-one forms of prayer. Regardless of the number, whatever form of prayer seems most natural to you can become an important instrument in overcoming your anxiety.

As a new mother, I occasionally became anxious and frustrated when my daughter cried and I couldn't soothe her. My mind would fill with negative thoughts about my expertise as a mother as well as all the things that could possibly be wrong with my child. These thoughts caused my body to tense and tighten. My anxiety and frustration served to make both of us more upset. When she was three weeks old, I remember praying, "Please God, make Reece stop crying." Then, I discovered a secret: Whenever she would start crying, I would sing the following prayer: "Praise the Lord for giving me Reece Louise. Praise the Lord, she's pretty as you please. Praise the Lord for Reece Barnett." The song prayer placed my focus not on my daughter's crying but on how she was a wonderful gift from God. My mind would clear, my body would relax, and my daughter would quickly soothe when I sang.

It's the same principle used in the book of Psalms, which are really song prayers. A song prayer moves your mind away from the upsetting anxiety-laden thought to a positive anxiety-free thought. As your mind becomes refocused, your physical anxiety dissipates. You are calmer in body and spirit. This calmness helps place you in control of the anxiety, as opposed to the anxiety controlling you.

Sometimes when you are in the midst of a particularly bad bout of anxiety, you forget how to pray. At this point it is important to ask or have someone pray with or for you. Praying with someone gives you support and comfort. Black women who suffer from panic and anxiety may feel as if they are all alone. When someone prays with you or you know someone is praying for you, this demonstrates that the belief is erroneous.

Prayer works. Over 191 scientific studies have proven it. Medical patients who pray or who are prayed for have a higher recovery rate than those who are not receiving prayers. In fact, the person does not have to know that someone is praying for them. The simple fact that you are being prayed for appears to make a difference. A recent study conducted at the Mid-America Heart Institute in Kansas City illustrates this point. One thousand heart patients who entered the institute's critical care unit were divided into two groups. Unbeknownst to the patients, one group received the prayers of a group of volunteers; the other group did not. In a one-year follow-up, the group that was prayed for had 11 percent fewer strokes, heart attacks, and life-threatening illness than the group that did not receive the sustained prayer. Prayer works.

When I talk to Black women who have overcome anxiety, most talk about how vital prayer was in the process. "I wouldn't be here if it wasn't for prayer," said Sharon. "Panic attacks had literally taken over my life. I felt as if I couldn't go on. A woman I barely knew from church came to see me. She told me that God told her to come. She prayed for me. That simple act of prayer gave me the strength and courage to go on. Seeing you on TV the next day was a direct answer to my prayer."

Many women mistakenly believe if they pray or have a group of people lay hands on them and pray, they will be instantly healed from anxiety. Over the past fifteen years I've interviewed two women whose anxiety recovery was an instant miracle, but in the majority of cases prayer advances the healing process. As women of faith it's important for us to remember that anxiety and fear directly affect our emotional health, and more often than not, emotional healing is a process. Prayer combined with CBT can be an integral part of the healing process.

Unless you are seeing a faith-based therapist or a member of the clergy, a topic discussed later in this chapter, your therapist will not pray with you during your therapy session. Given this certainty, the question becomes: How do you combine prayer and CBT? There are several ways. You can arrange to have people pray for you while you are in a therapy session. You can have someone pray with you before you go to the session. And similar to what I did with my daughter, you can turn prayer into positive self-talk or song. You can incorporate prayer into the homework that is such an integral part of CBT. Prayer is a proactive tool of your faith and, for an anxious, spiritual Black woman, a dynamic weapon in overcoming anxiety.

Before I close this section I want to interject a word of caution concerning prayer for Black women with OCD. Do not confuse prayer as part of the recovery process with prayer that is part of scrupulosity, the doubting form of OCD. If your prayer is in reaction to or a direct result of obsessive thoughts, it is a compulsion. Constant prayer and supplication to prevent something bad from happening or because you believe your sins have not been forgiven is nonproductive and keeps you stuck in the anxiety buildup and anxiety reduction cycle. If you find it too distracting to separate noncompulsive prayer from compulsive prayer, ask others to keep you in their prayers. Remember, studies show that having others pray for you works just as well as praying for yourself.

MEDITATIONS AND AFFIRMATIONS

Perhaps the most difficult thing for an anxious Black woman to do is be still and know. Stillness is the essence of meditation. Meditation is the act of disidentifying from inner thought flow and concentrating on calming and healing. When a woman meditates, she clears her mind and refills it with the positive written or spoken words of her faith. As she reflects on these words, she begins to experience a sense of peace. When one begins to meditate on a daily basis, these periods of calmness are extended. For the anxious Black woman these intervals serve as a form of relaxation. When one is in a calm, relaxed state, anxiety cannot enter.

Clarice learned the power of meditation in her Spiritual Way support group. During his own recovery, the group's facilitator, DaVonte, learned the power of mindfulness meditation. Now, he patiently taught the process to all members of the support group. As Clarice learned to stay in the moment and observe her thoughts and feelings in a detached, nonjudgmental way, she was amazed at the clarity of her thoughts. Mindfulness reduced her anxiety and fear, and gave her the courage to rebuild her life.

Mindfulness meditation, the form of meditation practiced in the Spiritual Way group, is extremely effective for women with anxiety difficulties. Developed by psychologist Jon Kabat-Zinn, mindfulness emphasizes a moment-to-moment awareness that is intentionally nonreactive and nonjudgmental. Several studies have shown that once women with panic attacks master and incorporate mindfulness into their daily lives, the level of anxiety is significantly reduced, and panic attacks decrease in number and severity. Mindfulness meditation has long-term benefits. Three years after being taught mindfulness, women who continued to practice it reported reduced anxiety levels.

During the course of any given day, Black women hear dozens of negative statements. If we refuse to accept these negative statements, our minds become blank. The human mind cannot remain in that state; it must fill itself with something. If there is nothing to take the place of the negative statements, our minds will begin to accept the statements, and eventually they will seep into our spirits.

Anxious women spend an inordinate amount of time receiving and dwelling on negative thoughts. As they learn to reject and release negative thoughts, they initially have difficulty filling their minds with positive ones. Faith-based affirmations provide these women with ready-made positive statements.

Affirmations are found in the Bible, the Koran, the teachings of Amenemopet, and the primary book of your faith. A favorite affirmation among the Christian Black women I work with is found in Philippians 4:13, "I can do all things through Christ who strengthens me." Websites and software programs are available that allow you to quickly pull out passages from the Bible or the Koran related to overcoming anxiety, fear, and worry. You can then make a list of these verses to use as positive self-statements. Once you compile your list, make copies of it and position them in places where you can readily see them. LaKeisha, the twin who worried, converted her affirmation sheet into a screensaver. The affirmations continuously scrolled across the screen of her home computer. Using another software program she created an affirmations calendar for her desk at work. The affirmations helped her manage her "what if" thoughts.

There are numerous books of affirmations on the market, and several are targeted for the African-American woman. These include Eric V. Copage's *Black Pearls: Daily Meditations, Affirmations, and Inspirations for African-Americans*; Dennis Kimbro's *Daily Motivations for African-American Success*; Patti LaBelle's *Patti's Pearls*; Stephanie Stokes Oliver's *Daily Cornbread: 365 Secrets for a Healthy Mind, Body, and Soul*; and Iyanla Vanzant's *Acts of Faith: Daily Meditations for People of Color*. Each book incorporates some element of faith in the affirmations. Each book can be easily tucked into a briefcase, purse, or backpack, to be carried with you throughout the day.

Affirmations play a crucial role in maintaining a life that is free from debilitating anxiety. They serve as the highest form of positive self-talk. The recently released "nun" study has shown positive statements, in written form, spoken form, and thoughts, play a vital role in helping women live a physically and emotionally healthy long life. In this study researchers examined the lives of retired nuns in their seventies, eighties, and nineties, from the time they first entered the convent as teenagers to the present day. Nuns who thought and spoke positive statements throughout their lives tended to be healthier and more active in their senior years. The relationship between positive statements and healthy aging was deemed so important *Time* magazine featured it as a cover story, and several other national publications and television news magazines featured the story.

As long as your anxiety difficulty is not OCD, it is okay if you read or repeat the same affirmation over and over again. The negative thoughts are repeating themselves in your head, so why not have something more positive repeating there?

MUSIC

Another tool of one's faith, music is quite effective in soothing both the physical and emotional aspects of anxiety. Inspirational music helps you to relax and loosens muscles that have tightened from worry. Remember the biblical story of David and his harp? Whenever King Saul was troubled and could find no peace, he called for David to play his harp. The notes that flowed from David's instrument soothed his soul. Music, as playwright William Congreve wrote in the seventeenth century, "has charms to soothe the savage breast, to soften rocks, or bend a knotted oak."

Callie, the college professor who encountered overt discrimination on the job, keeps a James Cleveland CD in her work computer. Whenever she feels anxiety begin to build, she clicks on "Peace Be Still." The words and music calm her. The calmness allows her to obtain clarity and insight into how to handle the racist incidents in a professional manner. "That CD makes such a difference," says Callie. "It helps me put things in the proper perspective and gives me the strength to handle the situation."

Callie's statement speaks to the healing power of gospel music. More than any music type, gospel appears to be a particularly effective tool for assisting Black women, regardless of their faith, with anxiety difficulties. Music may be used both in and outside the CBT sessions. Janise personalized the gospel song "We've Come This Far by Faith" as a positive self-statement during her gradual exposure sessions. Whenever she felt like leaving a social situation or taking a sip of vodka, she would quietly sing to herself, "Oh, oooh, oooh, can't turn around, I've come this far by faith."

The positive impact of gospel music on anxiety is so strong that I've incorporated it into the Soothe Your Nerves workshop. When the workshop musical director, Carla Davis, sings, tension drains from women's faces, muscles unfurl, and worries are forgotten. More important, workshop participants begin to believe they will get better. "I haven't stepped foot in a church since I was eighteen," wrote one participant. "But when your assistant started singing 'His Eye Is on the Sparrow,' I knew I was going to be all right." The impact is so strong that in our evaluations, participants ask us to include more musical selections.

Why does gospel music work to lessen anxiety? My friend Dr. Linda Walker, a music therapist and director of the Kent State University Gospel Choir, says that "whether in fast or slow tempo, with driving or smooth rhythms, gospel music elevates the spirit, speaks to the heart, and goes right to the soul."

FORGIVENESS

Anxious Black women are racked with shame and guilt. They believe they have somehow caused their anxiety by not having enough faith, by not living a better life, or by not being a better person. This belief is bolstered by the teachings in their various faiths. In the Christian tradition many Black women learn that "God has not given us a spirit of fear but of power and of love, and a sound mind" (2 Timothy 1:7). This verse has been interpreted to mean that fear and anxiety are not of God, so if you are experiencing problems with these two emotions, the problem lies with your relationship to God. Therefore, if you get right with God, you won't have an anxiety problem.

In the Yoruba belief system, anxiety and fear are not seen as dwelling within a person. Instead, these feelings of evil or ill ease are considered part of the outside physical world, where good and evil coexist. Anxiety and fear overtake a Black woman when she allows ill will to enter her life or is not paying attention to her spiritual self.

As Black women it is crucial that we understand that anxiety is not a sign of a lack or a lapse of faith. Nor does practicing a particular faith guarantee immunity from anxiety and fear. Christian, Catholic, Jew, Muslim, Buddhist, or Yoruba—debilitating anxiety is a nonsectarian experience.

On the surface, it would appear that Black women who cannot reconcile the need for therapy to assist in overcoming their anxiety with their spiritual beliefs have misinterpreted what it means to be a person of faith. From a spiritual perspective, the truth is a bit more complicated. In actuality, these women have not forgiven themselves for becoming anxious. By developing anxiety difficulties, they are convinced they have let everyone down, including themselves and their God.

"I can't believe I let this happen, Ang," Callie sobbed one day at lunch. "I'm a woman of faith. I'm a college professor. I have a Ph.D. I'm not supposed to have an anxiety problem. I feel like such a failure."

Callie's belief that she was entirely to blame for her anxiety problem only served to make her more anxious. Before she could move any further in overcoming her anxiety, she had to forgive herself. According to David A. Seamands, author of the book *Healing for Damaged Emotions*, forgiveness is the act of setting someone free from an obligation that is a result of a wrong done against you. Spiritually, forgiveness allows you to make peace with your past. It allows you to move forward into a new and better future. Forgiveness experts agree that it is easier to forgive someone else than to forgive yourself. This is especially true for Black women, who tend to hold themselves to a high and exacting standard.

The fact that Callie, or any Black woman for that matter, developed anxiety is not her fault. However, her response to her anxiety problem may have worsened it. Callie dealt with the anxiety by overeating, and this allowed her to avoid addressing the anxiety problem. Callie had to acknowledge her responsibility in the exacerbation of her anxiety problem. Then she had to forgive herself for that behavior. This simple, yet difficult act of forgiveness allowed Callie to rid herself of the shame and guilt. Once that happened, she was able to continue working through her anxiety problem. As an added bonus, once the shame and guilt were banished, Callie lost those last twenty-five pounds.

THERAPY IN THE FAITH

A well-trained CBT therapist will assist you in integrating the tools of your faith into your therapy session. But for some Black women, the fact that a CBT therapist will do that is not enough. Some of us will simply feel more comfortable receiving CBT from therapists who practice their spirituality in both their professional and personal lives. Such individuals are known as faith-based therapists.

One of the greatest blessings for anxious Black women is the increase in the number of well-trained faith-based psychologists, psychiatrists, and counselors. Several universities offer doctoral training in faith-based or spiritual psychology and counseling. Many divinity schools have master's programs in pastoral counseling. A small but significant number of Black psychologists and psychiatrists, after obtaining their doctorate or medical degree and license, receive fellowships to train with traditional Yoruba healers. Others go on to receive divinity degrees.

Faith-based therapists will blend the principles of your faith into every CBT session. Your session may begin and end with prayer, chanting, or meditation. Passages or examples from major books of your faith will be used in each session. Faith-based readings and activities will be part of your homework. Overcoming anxiety will be seen as a faith-building experience.

Churches, mosques, and other faith-based institutions may make therapy available to their members via lay counseling programs. Lay counselors are *not* professional therapists. The formal education of a lay counselor ranges from a high school diploma to a graduate degree. What most lay counselors have in common is a strong desire to minister to emotionally hurting people. A lay counselor's skills are honed in an intensive and extensive training program provided by the faith-based institution. Most lay counselors are trained for a year and a half before they officially become part of the institution's lay counseling program.

Lay counseling is brief—usually two to four sessions—and solution oriented. A reasonable goal for lay counseling is to reduce your anxiety to a level where you are able to decide on a more detailed plan of action for overcoming your anxiety difficulty. Should that plan include "professional" therapy, your lay counselor will help you find a good faith-based therapist. In fact, some lay counseling ministries have partnerships with faith-based psychology and counseling centers, and will arrange the initial appointment for you. Understand, however, that lay counseling is not a substitute for professional CBT. Lay counseling may help for a little while, but without CBT, your anxiety difficulty will quickly reemerge.

Several anxious Black women I know have sought help from spiritual advisers. In most cases the results were positive, but in one case it was a total disaster.

Shayla sought spiritual advice for her continuous cleaning behavior from a Pentecostal elder. He discerned that her compulsive cleaning behavior was due to an "unclean" spirit that inhabited her body, and he called upon several other elders to help him cast it out. They were unsuccessful. Disheartened and believing that the lack of success was her fault, Shayla made a near-fatal suicide attempt.

Shayla's experience was the exception, not the rule. There are many caring, competent, and wise spiritual advisers, but remember that spiritual advisers are neither professional nor lay therapists. A caring and gifted spiritual adviser is steeped in the wisdom of her faith and will help you think about the best course of action to take to overcome your anxiety. She will help you understand if things in your life are out of balance. She will offer you encouragement and direct you to examples in books of your faith that illustrate the fact that anxiety can be overcome. Most important, a wise spiritual adviser will work in tandem with your faith-based therapist to help you overcome your anxiety.

Beware of a spiritual adviser who tells you that the sole cause of your anxiety problem is an unclean spirit or demon and wants to cast it out or exorcise it. Make sure you clearly understand what the adviser is saying and what such a procedure will involve. Then seek another opinion, preferably from a faith-based psychologist or psychiatrist. No matter how debilitating the anxiety becomes, always remember that from a faith-based perspective, the roots of anxiety are psycho*spiritual*bio-social.

Just before I began to write this book, I spoke at a tiny church in the inner city. Recognizing the needs of the women in her pastorate, the pastor had asked me to set up a Soothe Your Nerves Sister Circle in the church. She introduced me to the congregation, and I said, "My name is Dr. Angela Neal-Barnett, and I am a clinical psychologist who specializes in anxiety disorders among Black women." The moment I finished that sentence, one of the old saints jumped up and yelled "Hallelujah," the organist hit a riff on the organ, and five women broke out in a holy dance. Ten minutes later, when I finally made my way back to my seat, my husband leaned over and whispered, "Well, finally you got in front of a congregation who understands that it's faith, hope, and therapy."

COGNITIVE BEHAVIOR THERAPY with a professional is one way to overcome anxiety; another option is self-help support groups. These are places for women who are experiencing anxiety to get together, share their triumphs and trials, and support and encourage one another. Support groups have always been a part of Black women's lives; we've just never called them by that name. Think back to the women who used to gather in your mother's kitchen to do hair or pray, or think of your own book clubs and sister circles. Each offered or offers support and encouragement for a group of Black women. Each in its own way was or is a support group.

For as long as I can remember, my mother has been part of a sister circle. She doesn't call it that; its official name is Prayer Coffee. Over the years I've watched the color of these women's hair change from brown and black to white and gray, and I've attended the funerals of many of them. Yet the bond between those still living remains as strong as ever. These women have supported one another through miscarriages, physical and mental illness, the deaths of husbands, the murder of a child, and getting children through law school, medical school, and a psychology Ph.D. program. Whenever I think about them, I am reminded of the awesome power that exists when Black women put their hearts and minds together.

Soothe Your Nerves Sister Circles tap into this natural power. These sister circles may take the place of professional therapy or be used in conjunction with therapy. Women within the sister circle who are not in therapy often find the courage and support to seek it out. Likewise, women who are in therapy find additional strength and support and, in concert with their therapist, make the mutual decision to end their professional therapy sessions.

Forming a sister circle is easy. Thousands of Black women are dealing with anxiety in some form and, as mentioned earlier, many believe they are the only one. The opportunity to talk and share with others who are experiencing the same thing is a blessing. You can simply post a flyer at the grocery store or online, place an announcement in a church bulletin or organization newsletter, or write a press release for the local paper. Be specific about the form of anxiety your sister circle plans to address. Give a telephone number or e-mail address that one can call or write for more information. In general, it is unwise to combine more than two types of anxiety in a sister circle. A Soothe Your Nerves Sister Circle for OCD should include only women with that anxiety problem.

Whereas it is easy to start a sister circle, maintaining and sustaining one takes time, planning, and commitment. The women who gathered in our mothers' or grandmothers' homes knew what they said in the kitchen stayed in the kitchen. They didn't expect to nor would they hear what they said repeated out in the neighborhood. No one signed a formal confidentiality statement; they'd known and trusted each other for years. In your own sister circle there will likely be women who know one another and some who do not. Therefore, it is important to set forth guiding principles of respect, trust, and confidentiality. These guiding principles should be stated at the beginning of each meeting. Too many sisters have been hurt because they spoke to another Black woman in confidence, only to have that person tell the neighborhood, school, office, mosque, or church.

The women of our mothers' generation also knew each other's personalities and shortcomings. In all likelihood this will not be the case in your sister circle. This raises the possibility that someone may want to participate or ends up participating in your sister circle who is inappropriate for the group. There are a variety of reasons why a woman may not be appropriate for your sister circle. She may be dealing with an anxiety difficulty that is different from the one that is the focus of the sister circle. Or she may have severe emotional problems in addition to anxiety difficulties; she may be angry and hostile and alienate herself; or she may be a know-it-all who is critical of everyone. Worst of all, she may violate the group's trust. The easiest way for sister circle organizers to avoid these problems is to screen each potential group member. This can be done by having women who are interested in the sister circle fill out an information sheet, which should be no longer than one page.

Here's a sample of a Soothe Your Nerves Sister Circle information sheet:

SOOTHE YOUR NERVES SISTER
CIRCLE FOR PANIC ATTACKS

Name _____ Age _____

Phone number where you can be contacted _____

E-mail address where you can be contacted _____

Type of anxiety experienced _____

How long have you experienced this anxiety difficulty?

How do panic attacks affect your life?

What do you hope to gain from participating in this group?

Have you ever participated in a self-help sister circle? If so, when
and where?

Are you currently a member of a sister circle self-help group?

Thank you for taking the time to fill out this information sheet.
—Angela Neal-Barnett, Sister Circle Organizer

As you review the information sheets, make sure the individual's anxiety difficulty is the same as the one or ones that will
be the focus of the group. Imagine how a woman with generalized anxiety disorder might feel in a sister circle where everyone
else is dealing with OCD?

As the sister circle's organizer, you want to make sure the
person doesn't already belong to two or three other self-help sister circles. Such an individual may be spreading herself too thin
or looking for answers that can be provided only in professional
therapy. You also want to make sure the potential member's ex-

pectations are realistic. Participation in the Soothe Your Nerves Sister Circle will not cure anyone's anxiety difficulty. What it will do is support and assist each member in her journey to overcome her anxiety difficulty.

Using an information sheet to screen potential members may not always be feasible. My Sunday morning sister circle is open to any woman in my church; I cannot screen out participants. Situations such as mine are the reason that guiding principles are essential to a sister circle. In almost every case when a member's behavior is detrimental to the sister circle, it is because she is violating a guiding principle. It is therefore important in the first session for the entire sister circle to determine what action will be taken if someone violates one of the guiding principles.

The Sunday morning sister circle decided that if someone did violate one of the principles, we would discuss it as a group and determine the impact it had on us as a group. If the person violated a principle a second time, then I as the group leader would privately ask the person not to return. No one ever violated a guiding principle.

Recently I spoke at a Soothe Your Nerves Sister Circle meeting where, earlier in the year, a member had been asked to leave. The group policy was that if a member violated a guiding principle, the group would discuss it and then vote on the appropriate course of action. But they also decided that no member would be left without support. If someone was asked to discontinue her participation, she would be given a list of professional therapy groups. The former member had violated the confidentiality of the other sister circle members. After discussing the incident and its impact, the women voted to dismiss her from the group. "It wasn't easy," shared one group member, "but our trust had been violated. If we were to continue, it was in the best interest of the group that she not be a member."

In my experience it is rare for someone to violate a guiding principle. The support and affirmation received and the skills learned in the sister circle are too precious for most members to jeopardize.

Finally, as a sister circle organizer, remember that while you are responsible for launching the group, the responsibility for maintaining the group lies with the entire group. Don't try to do everything. Increasing your stress often increases your anxiety. You'll end up burning out or undoing most of the progress you've made in overcoming your anxiety.

Once you have set your guiding principles, and members have been screened, use these ten general guidelines for organizing and facilitating your Soothe Your Nerves Sister Circle

SOOTHE YOUR NERVES SISTER CIRCLE

1. *Develop a mission statement.* It is very important for all group members to understand the purpose of the group. A mission statement clarifies the group's purpose. The group founders may develop the group's mission statement before the first meeting, or the entire group can develop it at the first meeting. Here is a sample mission statement:

   Mission Statement: To support and assist each other as we overcome_____(fill in the form of anxiety) using a psychological, spiritual, and Black perspective. The guiding principles of our sister circle are respect, trust, and confidentiality.

You may notice that I included the guiding principles in the mission statement. Doing so ensures that everyone is aware of and understands the purpose and ground rules of the group.

Each member should also develop her own personal mission statement. This statement reminds each woman why she chose to be a part of the sister circle. A personal mission statement strengthens each participant's commitment and connection to the sister circle. To assist group members in building their personal mission statements, have them complete the following two sentences:

> *I am here to_____.*
> *By doing so I will_____.*

Here's Clarice's personal mission statement from the Spiritual Way group: *I am here to learn how to live free of panic attacks and cocaine. By doing so I will be free to do the things I want to do with my life.*

Over time, members will find their personal mission statements changing and evolving. Encourage women to make written revisions of their mission statements. The changes reflect the new woman that is emerging as the anxiety difficulties are being overcome.

2. *Plan meeting times and places, and stick to the schedule.* The sister circle should meet at least once a month but no more than once a week. If the meetings are held at group members' homes, a different member should host each time. If you do not want to meet in homes, many community centers, libraries, and churches have rooms that can be used free of

charge; you just have to reserve the room. Be creative. I facil-
itate a sister circle during the Sunday school hour at my
church. Attendants include both church and non-church
members. Is there a college or university in your town with a
Black or Pan-African studies center or women's resource center? These centers often have space available free of charge
to community groups. My former university had a women's
resource center where we ran a sister circle for students and
women from the community.

One sister circle I am aware of meets at the community
recreational and wellness center. The women spend the first
part of the meeting walking two miles on the indoor track;
then they take a juice break and come together for the second part of the meeting. Setting the group up in this way
accomplishes two purposes: Walking is a form of exercise
that reduces anxiety and is physically healthy for them, and
the women begin the "talking" portion of their group in a
less anxious state.

Wherever you hold your meeting, food is optional. Don't
worry about cooking. Remember those "doing hair" parties?
All that was needed was a kitchen, a table, music, and a hot
comb. If you choose to have food, have everyone bring something. The hostess should provide the beverage. Remember:
no alcohol, caffeine, or chocolate.

Whether we are anxious or not, Black women are noto-
rious for running on CP time. Panic attacks, "what if" thinking, and compulsions often delay or prevent anxious women
from getting places. For this reason it is important that you
start and end your Soothe Your Nerves Sister Circle on time.
Knowing that the meeting will start without them or knowing that if they arrive after a certain time the meeting will be

over often gives sister circle members the extra courage needed to self-talk themselves through a panic attack or refrain
from engaging in the compulsion and make it to the meeting.

By the same token, don't beat up on people who are late.
If someone arrives after the meeting has started, simply
acknowledge her presence by saying, "We are so glad you're
here." Even if a member arrives five minutes before the meeting ends, acknowledge her presence. You'll soon find that CP
time becomes a thing of the past for most members of your
sister circle.

3. *Open each meeting by reading aloud the following quote:*

> *When I dare to be powerful, to use my strength
> in the service of my vision, then it becomes less
> important whether or not I am unafraid.*
> *— Audre Lorde*

It will remind members that they are not alone, that anxiety is treatable, and that they can reclaim their lives.

Provide background music that is inspiring and affirming. Absolutely no "bitch, ho, my man done gone" music
even if it does have a nice beat and is easy to dance to.
Gospel music is particularly effective. There are also wonderful jazz, R&B, and rap artists whose music speaks to the
spirits of Black women. Choose music that reflects different
genres and eras—artists such as India.Arie, Jill Scott,
Branford and Ellis Marsalis, Alicia Keys, Yolanda Adams,
and Sweet Honey in the Rock, to name a few. Carla Davis,
the musical director for my workshops, and I have developed
a play list of musical selections. We have included a few of

our favorites to help you get started. The members of your sister circle will help you fill in the rest.

SOOTHE YOUR NERVES MUSIC PLAYLIST

GOSPEL	R & B	JAZZ
"I Believe I Can Fly" by Yolanda Adams and Gerald Levert	"Video" by India.Arie	"Loved Ones" (an entire CD) by Ellis and Branford Marsalis
"We Fall Down" by Donnie McClurkin	"There's a Winner in You" by Patti LaBelle	"A Tisket, a Tasket" by Ella Fitzgerald
"Through It All" by Andrae Crouch	"A Rose Is a Rose" by Aretha Franklin	"Take the A-Train" by Duke Ellington
your sister circle's favorites	your sister circle's favorites	your sister circle's favorites

Designate a different person to be in charge of the music for each meeting. Try to have this person arrive early so that as the other sister circle members arrive, the music is already playing. By the time the meeting starts, members will already begin feeling uplifted and encouraged.

4. *Keep a journal.* Each member should keep a journal of her journey to recovery. Journaling allows you to see where you

are, where you've been, and where you are going in your quest to become anxiety free. Any bookstore or discount chain with a book section carries journals. I've even seen them next to the tabloids in the grocery store checkout line. The Sankofa Holistic Healing Institute in Oakland, California, has produced a journal specifically for anxious Black women. The Sankofa journal even has a place to write your daily affirmation. You can reach the institute by phone at 1-510-464-3035 or e-mail them at sankofahol@aol.com.

Have each member tape or glue a copy of her mission statement to the inside front cover of her journal. It will be the first thing she sees when she opens her journal and will remind her of her purpose in the sister circle and outside of it. Encourage members to bring their journal to the sister circle and share positive excerpts from it.

5. *Find a theme song.* No matter what her age, every Black woman I know has a song—a tune with words that encourages, uplifts, and helps her celebrate her success, reminds her of past or present love, or tells her story. A song that, when she hears it, makes her stop everything and say, "Excuse me, but I have to sing because they're playing my song." Just as you have songs for other aspects of your life, you need a song for the anxiety. It should be a song that you can sing on days when you are mastering your anxiety and a song you can sing on days when it seems the anxiety has mastered you.

When you find your theme song, write the words to it in your journal. Share your song with the other members of the sister circle. Designate one meeting as theme song day. Have everyone bring a CD or tape of her theme song. Play each sister's song and have her share how this song uplifts, encourages, or inspires her in her journey to overcome anxiety. Don't be surprised if at least once or twice during this meeting several sisters get up and start singing and dancing along, à la Diana Ross and the Supremes or Destiny's Child. While the sisters in your circle are deciding on their theme song, here is one of mine by Curtis Burrell that they can borrow.

> *"I Don't Feel No Ways Tired"*
>
> *I don't feel no ways tired,*
> *I come too far from where I started from,*
> *Nobody told me that the road would be easy,*
> *I don't believe He brought me this far to leave me.* *

6. *Share stories of Black women and men who have overcome or are overcoming anxiety.* Susan Taylor (publications director of *Essence* magazine), Beverly Johnson (model), Earl Campbell (Heisman Trophy winner and a former professional football player), and Bebe Moore Campbell (best-selling author) have all overcome panic attacks and anxiety. Share and discuss their stories in your sister circle. Campbell shares her story and the techniques she uses to manage her panic in the April 2002 issue of *Essence*. Taylor tells about her panic attack in her book, *In the Spirit*. Earl Campbell shares about his panic disorder in his autobiography, *The Earl Campbell Story: A Football Great's Battle with Panic Disorder.* Johnson tells her story on the GlaxoSmithKline website, and a video is available from the pharmaceutical company.

---

*Permission granted by Savoy Records/Savgos Music.

Everyone in your sister circle is overcoming a form of anxiety. Share your own stories. Use the following format:

1. My experience with anxiety began _____
2. The turning point for me was when _____
3. Currently, in the process of overcoming(fill in the form of anxiety), I am _____.
4. Over the next six months I want to be _____.
   By continuing to do_____and with the support and inspiration from my sisters in this circle, I believe I will achieve that goal.

The stories remind everyone that overcoming anxiety is not a straight line. There are ups and downs. But as your understanding of anxiety and the ways of mastering it grows, the down periods become shorter and the up periods become longer. Whether a celebrity story or your own, the stories are powerful and provide healing and inspiration to others in the sister circle.

7. *Practice the "so what" chorus.* The "so what" chorus is based on the Black church tradition of call and response. The exercise gives group members practice challenging and changing erroneous beliefs. A member shares a "what if" thought, and the other members respond in unison, "So what?" The member replies. Again the group responds. Do it ten times with each group member. Members may feel silly at first. So what? What is important is how group members feel at the end. The "so what" chorus helps everyone in the group deconstruct her erroneous beliefs by letting her state them and the emotion behind them. As each woman responds to the question "So what?" she begins to see how

she has catastrophized the situation. The "so what" chorus reminds women *that what we think will happen is far worse than what actually happens.*

Before doing this exercise, make sure you explain its purpose to the sister circle members. You may also want each member to read Chapter 8 of this book, to fully understand the purpose and importance of this activity.

8. *Visualize yourself anxiety free.* Visualization is a powerful tool in overcoming anxiety. Many members of your Soothe Your Nerves Sister Circle have spent months, even years, believing they would always be anxiety ridden or suffer from panic attacks. They cannot remember what it was like to be anxiety free. When we visualize, we replace the negative thoughts and images that are in our minds with positive thoughts and images. We give ourselves a picture of hope for the future.

In my Sunday morning sister circle I give each woman a mirror and a note card. On the note card I have members write a description of the woman they want to become; they tape this card to the mirror. Three times a day the women look into their mirror and see themselves as the woman on the card. Many of them begin the assignment somewhat reluctantly. They question how looking in a mirror is going to change anything. Usually by the second week they are eagerly doing the assignment. What's more, there is a noticeable difference in their attitude and demeanor. What makes the difference? Visualization. What the women in the sister circle see themselves becoming they believe they can become, and they begin to do the tasks to make it a reality. If your mind can conceive it and you can believe it, you will achieve it. This quote is from Napoleon Hill and is a favorite saying of the Reverend Jesse L. Jackson Sr. That's what happens in visualization: You begin to conceive, believe, and achieve. *Your mind is the most powerful tool you possess in overcoming anxiety.* Think of visualization as exercise and toning for the mind.

A VISUALIZATION EXERCISE FOR YOUR SISTER CIRCLE AND BEYOND

Each meeting, designate a different sister circle member to lead the visualization exercise. The first time the group does this exercise, place next to each group member's chair a 3-by-5-inch note card and a small frameless pocket mirror. (You can find these mirrors reasonably priced at craft or closeout stores.) Begin the exercise by playing soft instrumental jazz or inspirational music. Make sure everyone takes off their high heels and is sitting in a relaxed position. Take three slow, deep breaths and clear your mind. After the third breath, begin to visualize yourself anxiety free. If you experience panic attacks, visualize yourself panic free. See yourself grocery shopping, at your child's school play, and on the job—panic free. If social anxiety causes you difficulty, visualize yourself speaking in front of a small group or in a meeting asking for what you want, boldly and confidently. If OCD is your difficulty, see yourself going about your daily routine without engaging in compulsive behavior. If you have generalized anxiety, visualize a completely worry-free day. Whatever form your anxiety takes, see yourself doing the things you want to do. As you watch yourself doing these things, note the expression on your face, your posture, and the lack of tension in your muscles.

After completing the visualization exercise, ask each member to record what she visualized on the note card. Then have each one tape the note card to the inside back cover of her journal. Next, have the women affix the mirror above the note card with rubber cement. Instruct your sister circle members to open the back of the journal twice a day—when they get up in the morning and when they go to bed at night—to read their vision, look in the mirror, and visualize themselves as that woman.

9. *Invite guest speakers.* Every third meeting invite a professional from the community to talk about a topic related to overcoming anxiety. Speakers may include relaxation specialists, spa directors, psychologists, psychiatrists, herbalists, massage therapists, and stress management consultants. They will be more than happy to come. In fact, they may invite your group to meet at their establishment and give each of you a complimentary service.

    Is there a speaker you want to bring in but can't afford? Ask your local chapter of the Association of Black Psychologists, National Medical Association, National Black Accountants, Links, or sorority graduate chapters to cosponsor the event. By doing so you widen the circle of Black women who become educated about anxiety. Do you know a pharmaceutical representative? Pharmaceutical companies often cosponsor talks, complete with appetizers and beverages. On more than one occasion I've spoken to sister circles that have partnered with other groups to sponsor my workshop.

10. *Close each meeting with an affirmation circle.* Stand or sit in a circle holding hands. Go clockwise around the circle and

have each woman repeat her favorite affirmation. Another option is to read an inspirational poem in the round. Again, going clockwise, have each woman read a verse or line of the poem aloud. Maya Angelou's "Phenomenal Woman" and "And Still I Rise," and Gloria Wade Gayles's "Anointed to Fly" and "And the Women Gathered" are four poems that I have found work well in the round. Whether you use affirmations or poems, the impact is extraordinary.

Soothe Your Nerves Sister Circles make a difference in anxious Black women's lives. Tee organized a sister circle for Black women with panic attacks by placing an announcement in her sorority alumnae newsletter. Eight women responded. Based on their information sheets, all were appropriate for the group. The group meets monthly in a room at the community center. All agree that the group has changed their lives. "I realize that by putting this sister circle together, I'm not just helping others, I'm helping myself," said Tee. "The support from my sorors is fantastic."

"I agree," said Selena. "I was taking medication for the panic attacks, but it wasn't helping much. The visualization exercises made a profound difference in my life. I realized that if I was to become the woman I saw myself as becoming, I would need professional CBT. The sisters in the group were supportive and encouraging. My therapist wants to know how he can start a sister circle."

"For me it was the music," said Lela. "I chose as my theme song 'Ain't Gonna Let Nobody Turn Me Around.' Not long after that when I was in Nordstrom, I began to feel a panic attack coming on. I started humming that song. It cleared my mind and allowed me to focus on my self-statements. Before, I would have run out of the store, but this time I just kept shopping."

The biggest endorsement for the sister circle came from an unlikely source: the director of the community center where the group held their monthly meetings. When Selena went in early one evening to set up the music, the director stopped her and wanted to know what went on in there. She said we didn't look like the same women; we seemed more peaceful, calm, and confident. "So I looked her straight in the eye and told her exactly what was going on," said Selena. "In that room, sisters are doing it for themselves."

ELEVEN

A S THE STORIES THROUGHOUT this book illustrate, anxiety disrupts the lives of Black women. It separates them from their husbands, lovers, children, parents, siblings, and friends. Many times the spouses and lovers leave or threaten to leave. They don't stop loving the person; it just becomes very difficult, if not impossible, to live with them. It becomes harder and harder for friends and family members to keep up with the needs, desires and demands of anxious Black women. But we try because we consider ourselves loyal, loving friends and family members. The result often is burnout and the need to remove ourselves from that particular person's life.

"I just can't take it anymore," said Ron. "I love Isabelle, but her praying and candle lighting is driving me crazy." Ron and Isabelle met at a historically Black college in New Orleans. Both were Black Catholics who took their faith seriously. When they were dating, Ron noticed that Isabelle liked things neat and orderly; there was a special place for everything in her dorm room. Since they'd been married, however, it seemed as if she was always arranging things, working her rosary beads, or lighting candles. Some nights she was so busy praying she didn't come to bed until 2 A.M. They'd been married only six months!

Ron is not alone. Many spouses and significant others have confided to me that they are seriously considering leaving. They are simply at their wit's end as to how to deal with the other person's anxiety, which seems to disrupt every aspect of their life.

Melody and Marquis had been together so long, people considered them married. When they first met, Melody was a registered nurse and Marquis was a DJ and part-time rapper. With Melody's support, encouragement, and financial backing, he enrolled at the local university and later graduated with a degree in communications. Within a year Marquis was a member of a local TV station's early-morning news team. He believed that without Melody he'd still be spinning records for Soul Night at the VFW. Melody believed in him when no one else did. He could talk about anything with her.

During Marquis's first year at the television station, Melody began to experience panic attacks when driving over bridges; then driving itself became difficult. At first Marquis didn't mind driving her to work; he figured it would be for only a little while. As the months wore on, he became increasingly upset with Melody; she wanted him to drive her everywhere! She was no longer interested in his plans and his life; all she was interested in was herself and not driving. He couldn't talk to her anymore without getting into an argument. This was not the woman he'd fallen in love with; in fact, he wasn't even sure he liked this new Melody.

When one is in a relationship with an anxious Black woman, the boundaries and roles in the relationship shift. A relationship that has been a mutual give and take changes to one where it feels as if the anxious woman is doing all the taking and the spouse or significant other is doing all the giving. If the relationship is one where prior to the anxiety the woman was doing the lion's share of the giving, the change in roles can be quite jarring and in some cases cause the end of the relationship.

That's what happened to Marquis and Melody. Their whole relationship had changed: The independent, confident Melody was gone, and in her place was a clingy, dependent woman. But Marquis had invested too much in the relationship to let a specific phobia and cued panic attacks destroy it. He approached me in the green room after I appeared on a segment of his morning news show. I was able to give him the names of several therapists who specialize in treating specific phobias. In addition, I gave him my website address, www.risesallyrise.com, which includes a page for family and friends of anxious Black women.

EVERYTHING WILL BE ALL RIGHT

Living with an anxious Black woman is challenging. Part of the challenge stems from the fact that many of the things that seem natural to do with an anxious Black woman do her more harm than good.

When Melody first became fearful of driving over bridges, Marquis lavished her with reassurances. "Honey, I know everything's going to be okay," he told her. "You've driven over bridges since you were sixteen. You know there is nothing to be afraid of." Marquis's reassurances didn't seem to help the situation, and before long Melody didn't want to hear them.

It is natural to want to reassure the person that everything

will be all right. "There's nothing to worry about," "I'm here for you," "I won't leave you," and "Everything is going to be okay" are phrases often used by family and friends to calm an anxious person. However, when anxiety is controlling a Black woman's life, reassurances do not work. The reason they don't work is that they don't give the anxious Black woman power over the anxiety. It's like trying to reassure a small child who comes into her parents' bedroom and says there is a monster under her bed. No matter what the parents say, they can't get her to believe there is no monster. They can give the child all the reassurance in the world, and she will still end up sleeping in their bed. But one of the things that every child knows is that monsters hide under beds because they don't like light. So, if the parents give the child a flashlight to shine under the bed, they give her power over the monster.

Like the small child, rather than reassurance, the anxious Black woman needs a flashlight—words and actions that help her gain power or mastery over the anxiety. As friends and family we can help them develop these words and actions, but we cannot do it for them, nor can we force them to do it for themselves. The latter is a strategy many of us try to employ. "I know if she would just try harder, she would get over this" is a common refrain uttered by loved ones. In actuality, helping an anxious Black woman overcome anxiety is not about getting her to try harder. It is about giving her the tools to develop the courage and strength to face the anxiety and fear. When an anxious Black woman faces her anxiety, she learns that what she thought or imagined would happen is far worse than what actually happens. She gains the courage to face the anxiety and fear again. As a Black woman develops courage, she learns, as Dr. Susan Jeffers has written, to feel the fear and do it anyway.

Before we can offer our anxious loved one a flashlight, we must gain insight into our own feelings and understand how those feelings impact our interactions with our anxious loved one. It is only when we understand ourselves and our own reactions to the anxiety that we can begin the process of helping a loved one overcome anxiety.

FRUSTRATION AND ANGER

Frustration is the most common emotion experienced by families, spouses, significant others, and friends of anxious Black women. Family and friends remember how the woman—their wife, girlfriend, sister, daughter, or friend—used to be and want that woman back. They are baffled as to why the other person can't get over it, especially if she is in therapy. "I thought seeing a psychologist was supposed to help Isabelle get better," said Ron, "but she seems worse."

Part of Ron's frustration stems from his lack of understanding of OCD. Isabelle has been plagued by obsessive-compulsive difficulties for years. Change will not occur overnight or in a couple of therapy sessions. As part of her therapy Isabelle is being asked to let go of behavior she has engaged in for many years and replace it with something new and unknown. That's scary. Most people when given the choice between what is known and what is unknown stick with what is known. In the first stages of overcoming OCD, an increase in the compulsions is to be expected. Both Ron and Isabelle must remember that as Isabelle practices letting go of the compulsive behavior, the less anxious she will become. But the hardest part is the beginning.

Ron's frustration level dropped significantly when he took time to educate himself about OCD. Suddenly it was no longer

Isabelle's "praying problem" but OCD. He had a better understanding of what to expect in the therapy process. Reading about the behavior gave him ideas about what he could do to support Isabelle during the process.

For spouses and lovers, sexual intimacy is a particularly sensitive source of frustration. Anxious Black women tend to withdraw from sexual activity. Women with panic attacks curtail sex for fear of having a panic attack in the middle of a sex act. The physical sensations experienced during lovemaking—increased heart rate, shallow breathing, tingling, and sweating—are similar to those of a panic attack. Anxious women are unable to distinguish the characteristics of being aroused from the symptoms of a panic attack. Women with OCD may have obsessive thoughts intrude at an inopportune point in the lovemaking process. Isabelle would experience repetitive thoughts of unpardonable sin during foreplay and abruptly leave to go light candles, leaving Ron frustrated and bewildered. Women with contamination fears may use double and triple forms of protection to prevent a spread of germs. They may also shower zealously after intercourse. Women with generalized anxiety may experience difficulties deriving pleasure from lovemaking. It becomes difficult to enjoy sex or fake like you're enjoying sex if during the activity you are worried about 101 different things. In addition, the tightness and tension associated with generalized anxiety may at times make penetration difficult and painful.

Friends and family members who are frustrated must gain an understanding of the power of fear. The fear associated with various forms of anxiety is so intense that most women would rather avoid it than feel and work through it. Avoidance is easier and eliminates the risk of anything bad occurring. In other words, anxious women reason that if they do nothing, nothing will happen. But they are wrong. Doing nothing increases an anxious woman's level of anxiety. It also increases the frustration level of those who love her.

Unresolved frustration frequently gives way to anger. My workshop Bad Nerves or What? is specifically designed for family and friends of anxious Black women. At a recent workshop, June, a woman in the audience, shared how angry she was with her ex–best friend Olivia, who suffered from panic attacks and agoraphobia. June had recently turned thirty, and her family threw a huge party. Olivia had promised she would be there, but she never showed. Although June knew Olivia suffered from panic attacks and knew that the attacks sometimes prevented her from going places, she never imagined her best friend would miss her thirtieth birthday party. Needless to say, June was hurt and angry. "She could have come if she wanted to," she said bitterly.

Anger is dangerous because it is often misplaced, and misplaced anger helps no one. Misplaced anger is detrimental to those who are experiencing and nursing it, and it is harmful to the anxious woman at whom it is directed. Please note that I said "misplaced anger." As friends, spouses, and significant others, it is all right for us to be angry. We just must be very clear in our mind what we are angry about and make sure we express that anger appropriately. Many people mistakenly believe they are angry *at* the anxious person. In many cases they are angry *about* the anxiety difficulty that has turned their friend, lover, family member, or spouse into a person they barely know. As the workshop progressed, June recognized her anger was misplaced. She wasn't mad at Olivia; she was mad that panic and agoraphobia had taken control of Olivia's life. During the workshop she practiced expressing her anger to Olivia. Using the monster under the bed analogy, the workshop's participants generated ideas about the types of flashlights Olivia could give June. The next week, June e-mailed me with an update:

> Dear Dr. Barnett:
> I spoke with Olivia and told her how angry and disappointed I was that she missed my party. I also told her how angry I was about the panic and agoraphobia that had taken control of her life. I told her that I was angry about the person she had become because of the anxiety. I told her about your workshop and how you said people with panic can reclaim their life. She started crying and said she felt like everyone blamed her for not trying harder, and this was the first time any friend or family expressed anger over what had happened. To make a long story short, she talked to her psychiatrist about cognitive behavior therapy, and he referred her to someone. She starts in two weeks. I'll keep you posted.
> —June (the lady with the misplaced anger)

The two most detrimental things you can do is keep your anger bottled up inside or go off. You must acknowledge your anger and find a common ground on which you and your loved one can agree. This common ground may simply be "Yes, the anxiety is wreaking havoc with our relationship." If you start yelling and screaming, you will only become angrier. If you suppress your anger, it will eventually express itself in a way that is detrimental to you, detrimental to the anxious person, and detrimental to the relationship you share.

That is what happened to the twins, LaNeisha and

LaKeisha. Prior to signing up for my workshop series, they had a huge fight over LaKeisha's inability to stop worrying. Taking the workshop classes was a way for both of them to find out what kind of help was available for the worry and begin to heal the rift in their relationship.

SHE'S JUST FOOLING YOU

One question I am asked at every workshop I conduct is "Aren't there women who use their anxiety and fear to control people?" Absolutely. Some women with anxiety difficulties are manipulative and use their anxiety to gain attention and sympathy, and to keep people close. Let's be honest: Who among us wouldn't want their entire circle of friends and family catering to their every whim? But the vast majority of anxious Black women are frightened and scared, and want to get better. If you believe a woman is using her anxiety difficulties to manipulate you, examine your responses to her anxious behavior. Does the way you respond reinforce the manipulative, controlling behavior? For example, when she says she's beginning to have a panic attack, do you drop everything and rush to her side? If you're scheduled to go out for the evening and she's tense and worried, do you cancel your plans? Such responses on your part reinforce the anxiety and manipulation on her part. If you find your responses reinforce the manipulation, you must learn to change your responses. Otherwise, you are not helping your anxious loved one, and you are certainly not helping yourself.

Initially, learning to change her response was hard for LaNeisha. After all LaKeisha was her twin. As the workshop progressed, both women recognized that at times LaKeisha used her anxiety to manipulate LaNeisha. "I don't mean to," said

LaKeisha, "I'm just so afraid that she's going to give up on me, too. She's my best friend and my twin, and if she leaves, I'll have nobody." "That's what makes it so hard," responded LaNeisha. "She's my twin. If I don't help her, who will? But sometimes it feels as if I'm giving up too much of my own life."

Despite her misgivings, LaNeisha decided to work on changing responses. Six weeks after the workshop ended, LaNeisha came in for a follow-up session. "You were right," she said. "Changing my response really helped improve my relationship with my sister. Rather than getting angry or doing things for her, I just use the 'so what' chorus, but I guess in my case it's a 'so what' solo. What's important is I'm not giving into manipulation, and I'm helping myself and my sister."

RESENTMENT AND DISBELIEF

Isabelle and Olivia shared their anxiety difficulties with at least one other person. In most cases it's not easy for an anxious Black woman to share her experiences. This is partly due to our beliefs about how Black women should handle difficulties. For a Black woman to admit that she is being controlled by anxiety is akin to giving up membership in the Strong Black Woman's club. A second reason is fear of the reaction of friends and loved ones. What will they think of me? Will it change what they think of me? Will they still love me? Will they leave me? All these questions cross the minds of anxious Black women.

Remember Tee, the woman in Chapter 2 who experienced panic attacks? When she began to overcome her panic attacks, she shared her experience with her husband, Keith. Hurt and confused, he said, "Do you mean to tell me I'm married to a crazy woman?"

Many of you reading this book probably think Tee's husband is insensitive and are sending evil thoughts his way. On the surface, his comment confirms every anxious Black woman's worst fear. But give the man a break; in actuality his comment is normal. As friends and family members we have little experience with anxiety. Black folks don't talk about it. Black magazines rarely write about it. Aretha doesn't sing about it. We just don't know.

For Black women in the midst of overcoming anxiety, there are two responses to the husband's remark: get stressed out, become more anxious, and begin to experience panic symptoms, or recognize that the response is coming from a lack of knowledge and fear.

Tee chose the latter. "I can see how you might think that. At first I thought that, too, but it is not true," she told her husband. "People who suffer from panic attacks and anxiety are not crazy. Here's some information on panic attacks. Let's sit down and look it over together." They did. As Tee shared, Keith took her hand, looked in her eyes, and said, "Baby, why didn't you tell me about this earlier? I could have helped."

THE THREE MOST IMPORTANT THINGS

Frustration, anger, and disbelief are the three most common emotions experienced. If you are a family member or friend and have experienced any or all of these emotions, you are normal. The key is to experience and express them in ways that are productive and healthy for you and productive for your anxious loved one. To do so, you must do the following three things.

1. *Educate yourself about the various forms of anxiety.* First and foremost, as friends, lovers, and spouses, you must know

that what you are dealing with is more than a case of bad nerves. Your loved one is suffering from anxiety, and it is important to educate yourself about the specific form of anxiety she has. Like Isabelle's husband, Ron, you must call it by its right name. In doing so, you demystify the condition and eliminate the stigma and secrecy between yourself and your loved one. You also establish a firm foundation to assist your loved one in overcoming anxiety or help her seek assistance for overcoming anxiety. This book provides family members with a good understanding of the various forms of anxiety and the help available to overcome them.

2. *If you choose to help your loved one overcome anxiety and fear, remember to encourage and support, but don't enable.* Anxious friends and loved ones get better because they gain mastery or control over their anxiety. Allowing her to avoid the feared event, experience, or person—or trying to protect your friend or loved one from them—only serves to make matters worse. Allowing the woman's anxiety to control your life is also a form of enabling. A simple rule of thumb is to check your responses to your loved one's anxious behavior. If your response makes you feel angry, bitter, or frustrated, more than likely you are enabling. As LaNeisha learned, changing your responses to your loved one's anxiety doesn't just help you, it also helps her.

3. *Be true to yourself.* First, take care of yourself. The major mistake made by caregivers is self-neglect. You are so busy trying to meet the other person's needs that you forget your own. The bottom line is that you cannot help anyone overcome anxiety if you are a mess. Set aside at least a half hour

each day just for you, and stick to it. It may be something as simple as sitting in a room by yourself, sipping a cup of tea, or locking the bedroom door and taking a nap.

Ron, Marquis, June, and LaNeisha had to learn to put themselves first. Putting yourself first does not make you an uncaring, coldhearted person. What it does do is place you in the position to support and encourage your spouse, significant other, sister, or friend. Remember to speak the truth, but speak it with love and understanding. Lying or keeping information from your anxious friend or loved one does not help, and in the end the truth will come out, sometimes in ways you have no control over.

WHAT ABOUT THE CHILDREN?

So far we've talked about adults' reactions to loving and living with an anxious Black woman, but what about the children? Last year I witnessed as a parent rather than a psychologist the impact of an anxious mother on her child.

Lamont was a member of my daughter's class; so was his mother. Lamont's mother was so terrified that something bad was going to happen to Lamont that she never left his side and carried him everywhere. During the first semester of preschool, I never saw Lamont walk; I assumed he couldn't. Much later I found out my assumption was incorrect. Lamont could walk, but his mother just wouldn't allow it.

During the first three months of preschool, Lamont's mother remained in the classroom every day, all day. I didn't find this out until we received the school picture. My daughter took one look at the class picture and exclaimed, "Hey, Lamont's mommy is missing!" "Sweetie," I said gently, "Lamont's mommy is not in your class." "Yes, she is, Mommy. She's there all the time." The next day I mentioned to Lamont's mother what my daughter had said. "Oh, yes," she replied uneasily. "Lamont has a nervous problem."

As I observed Lamont's mother over the school year, she appeared to be experiencing both generalized anxiety and social anxiety difficulties. She was so worried that something horrible would happen to Lamont, she would not leave him by himself. Lamont never became comfortable with the other children in class because his mother wouldn't let him interact with them. While the other children napped in the nap room, Lamont's mother placed his cot in the hallway. At lunchtime he and his mother sat at a table by themselves. During family nights Lamont and his mother did not interact with the other parents.

Eventually the school counselor told Lamont's mother that they would help her become comfortable with leaving Lamont alone in the classroom with the head teacher, associate teacher, two student teachers, two practicum students, and the two graduate students who occupied the observation booth. Upon hearing this information, she immediately pitched a fit and had a full-blown panic attack. By March they succeeded in getting her to leave Lamont in the classroom for four hours. This lasted for two weeks. Sitting at home, her mind flooded with worry: What if Lamont needed her? What if something happened to Lamont? What if the school couldn't reach her? She began to experience panic attacks. Lamont's mother returned to the classroom, where she remained until school ended. Lamont is not returning to preschool. His mother told me, "It just wasn't working out."

Lamont's mother projected her anxiety difficulties onto Lamont. Although she was the one who was suffering from anxiety, she told everyone including herself that Lamont had the problem. As the therapist was weaning her away from the class-room, Lamont began to blossom. He sang and danced with the other children, walked everywhere, and began taking naps in the nap room. But all that stopped when his mother returned to the classroom.

Lamont's mother represents one end of the continuum of anxious Black mothers. Anxious Black mothers on the other end of the continuum try to hide their anxiety problems from their children; by doing so they believe they are protecting the children. Despite their efforts, children are aware that something is wrong. They recognize their mother doesn't go places or do many things with them. They observe the compulsive behavior and the chronic worry. Children express their awareness of their mother's anxiety in direct and indirect ways. Some may ask, "Mommy, why are you scared?" Others may express it in their play or take on the parent's anxious symptoms.

The day Tee contacted me, she had overheard her seven-year-old daughter playing with her dolls. "Now Mommy's scared. So just Daddy and Ally will go to church," she said. "It was at that moment I knew I had to get better," Tee said. "If not for me, then for my children."

Children who are kept in the dark about their parent's anxiety often feel unloved and unwanted. These feelings stem from their observations that their mothers don't do the same things that other kids' mothers do. Various anxiety difficulties may keep Black mothers from attending their children's school and social functions. Or if they do attend, the mothers are so anxious that they don't let the child fully participate. Because they know something is wrong, children mistakenly believe that whatever causes their mother to act that way is their fault.

As a psychologist, I often wonder what Lamont thought as

he sat on his mother's lap, apart from the other children. While the other children were romping and running or singing and dancing, Lamont's mother just seemed to hold him tighter.

Children of anxious parents are at higher risk to develop anxiety difficulties. As we learned in Chapter 1, the reason for this is biopsychosocial. Children may inherit a predisposition for anxiety. Additionally, they may learn anxious behavior from observing their parents. It is not unusual to hear the child of an anxious mother say, "Mommy's scared to go outside, and I am, too."

WHAT DO I TELL THE CHILDREN?

With children, the best course of action is to tell the truth. It is important to remember, however, that children need the simple truth, not a long-drawn-out clinical explanation. Children's questions should be answered simply and directly, and in terms they can understand. When explaining OCD to her daughter, Shakira, Tamika said, "Sweetie, do you know why Mommy checks the doors so many times before we leave the house? It's because she has something called obsessive-compulsive disorder. Obsessive-compulsive disorder is like the hiccups. You know how when you get the hiccups it's hard to stop? Well, when I start checking the doors, it's also hard to stop." One of the first questions Shakira asked was "Will I get obsessive-compulsive disorder, too?" "No, honey," Tamika answered. "Obsessive-compulsive disorder is not something you catch like a cold." "Will you get better?" Shakira asked. "Yes, honey, I will get better." "I'm glad, Mommy," Shakira said. "I love you." Tamika's conversation with Shakira demonstrates that the simple answer will suffice.

Your children will not think less of you because of your

anxiety. More often than not they will try to help. When Tee told Ally about being scared sometimes, Ally replied, "That's okay, Mommy. Sometimes I get scared, too."

Sharing the simple truth with your child helps dispel the feelings of being unloved and unwanted. Some uninformed children believe they are the reason that their mother doesn't do things with them. Such beliefs may result in the child's experiencing sadness and low self-esteem.

In almost all cases, once you begin the process of overcoming anxiety, letting your children know what is happening is a positive thing. Sharing with your children helps them articulate their own fears and concerns. They also learn that it is okay to be scared and that you can conquer fear and anxiety difficulties.

Family and friends are vital to the process of overcoming anxiety. Being supported and having someone in your corner gives you additional resources to draw on. But please remember, the most important person in this journey is you, aided by your faith in a spiritual power, your vision of an anxiety-free self, and your belief that you can master your anxiety.

Along this journey there will be times when you become afraid that you will never get better and want to give up. Don't. Instead, remember that within you lies the strength and courage to overcome anxiety and reclaim your life.

RESOURCES

❖

Numerous organizations, books, tapes, and videos exist to assist you in overcoming anxiety. Your most valuable resource in your journey to overcome anxiety, however, is you and your desire to no longer allow anxiety to control your life. This desire is the reason you read this book. It is what will sustain you as you take your next step to soothe your nerves. Believe in this desire and, more important, believe in yourself. The more you do, the easier the journey becomes.

THE PUBLIC LIBRARY

The public library provides access to most of the resources listed in this book. Today's library doesn't just have books; it has CDs, cassette tapes, and videos. What's more, as a library cardholder you are entitled to Internet access. If you don't have a computer at home, you can access the Websites from the library of all the organizations listed in this chapter. You can access my Website, www.risesallyrise.com, and send me an e-mail at drbarnett@risesallyrise.com.

The public library will help you maintain and sustain your Soothe Your Nerves Sister Circle. Rather than going out and buying affirming music for your meeting, you can borrow the CDs or cassette tapes from the library. Don't forget to return them! My local library even carries the Beverly Johnson video-tape on panic disorder.

If you don't have a library card, they are very easy to ob-tain. Most libraries will issue you one for free. Others, particu-larly those in big cities, may charge a nominal fee. The access to information you gain is priceless.

BUILDING A PERSONAL RESOURCES LIBRARY

Soothe Your Nerves is the first book in your personal anxiety resources library. As you learn to overcome and manage your anxiety, you will add more books to your collection. What's great about owning the books is that you can highlight passages and write notes in the margins without other people getting upset.

When you contact the organizations listed in this chapter or access their Websites, you will find many of them offer free booklets and fact sheets on the various forms of anxiety. Go ahead and request these free materials.

Before long you will find that your personal library contains a number of books, pamphlets, and other resources that can be shared with anxious women who are where you once were: losing hope and feeling as if they are the only ones. By sharing your re-sources you are also helping yourself. For women who are over-coming anxiety, helping others is an effective way of preventing a major relapse or working through a temporary setback.

ORGANIZATIONS

American Psychological Association (APA)
750 First Street, NE
Washington, DC 20002-4242
Phone: 800-374-2721
www.apa.org

This is the nation's oldest and largest association for psychologists. The APA's Office of Publication Information provides data on anxiety disorders. You can also obtain the address and phone number of your state's psychological association and licensing board from the APA.

Anxiety Disorders Association of America
8730 Georgia Avenue, Suite 600
Silver Spring, MD 20910
Phone: 240-485-1035
www.adaa.org
E-mail: AnxDis@ada.org

The executive director of this organization also overcame panic disorder. ADAA provides information, brochures, books, and tapes on various forms of anxiety. It also keeps a list of professional therapists around the country who specialize in anxiety treatment. You can call the organization to request the names of therapists in your area. Make sure you specify that you are looking for someone who uses CBT or if you specifically want a Black or multicultural therapist. ADAA holds an annual conference at the end of March or the beginning of April that includes a series of workshops and lectures for people overcoming anxiety difficulties.

Association for the Advancement of Behavior Therapy (AABT)
305 Seventh Avenue
New York, NY 10001
Phone: 212-647-1898
www.aabt.org

AABT is the home organization for a special interest group of Black cognitive behavior therapists. The organization also has a special interest group of multicultural and cross-cultural therapists. E-mail or call the organization for a list of CBT therapists in your area. The organization also has fact sheets on various forms of anxiety.

Association of Black Psychologists (ABPsi)
P.O. Box 55999
Washington, DC 20040-5999
Phone: 202-722-0808
www.abpsi.org

The national organization for Black psychologists, ABPsi provides a referral service. Call to receive the names of Black psychologists in your area who treat anxiety difficulties.

Black Psychiatrists of America
c/o Ramona Davis, M.D.
866 Carlston Ave.
Oakland, CA 94610
Phone: 510-834-7103

Fax: 415-695-9830

www.blackpsychiatristsofamerica.com

This national organization is committed to the mental health needs of Black Americans.

Freedom from Fear
308 Seaview Avenue
Staten Island, NY 10305
Phone: 718-351-1717
www.freedomfromfear.com

This organization does wonderful outreach into Black and Latin communities. Freedom from Fear also provides a listing of research studies by state where free anxiety treatment is available. The organization's founder and executive director overcame twenty-five years of panic disorder, agoraphobia, and depression.

National Black Women's Health Project
600 Pennsylvania Avenue SE, Suite 310
Washington, DC 20003
Phone: 202-548-4000
Fax: 202-543-9743
www.nationalblackwomenshealthproject.org
Email: nbwhp@nbwhp.org

This organization is specifically devoted to Black women's emotional and physical health. Booklets and videos are available. The organization takes a grassroots approach to Black women's health.

National Institute of Mental Health (NIMH)
Anxiety Disorders Education Program
Office of Scientific Information
5600 Fishers Lane, Room 7-99
Rockville, MD 20857
Phone: 1-888-ANXIETY
www.nimh.nih.gov/anxiety

NIMH has numerous booklets, videos, and information about treatment research studies available on panic attacks and other forms of anxiety. The materials are available for free or for a nominal fee and are a treasure trove for Soothe Your Nerves Sister Circles and personal resource libraries. Call the toll-free number to find out what is currently available.

National Medical Association
1012 Tenth Street, NW
Washington, DC 20001
Phone: 202-347-1895
www.nmanet.org

The National Medical Association is committed to the physical and emotional health needs of African Americans. A physicians' referral service is available through their Website. You can locate Black psychiatrists in your area.

National Mental Health Association
1021 Prince Street
Alexandria, VA 22314-2971
Phone: 1-800-969-NMHA
www.nmha.org

One of the oldest consumer-based mental health organizations, NMHA has 340 affiliate offices across the United States in addition to a national office. Call the national office to find out if there is a local affiliate in your area. Your local affiliate can suggest speakers for your Soothe Your Nerves Sister Circle.

Obsessive-Compulsive Foundation, Inc.
337 Notch Hill Road
North Branford, CT 06471
Phone: 203-315-2190
www.ocfoundation.org
E-mail: info@ocfoundation.org

This organization is dedicated to educating people about obsessive-compulsive disorder. The executive director is a lawyer who has learned to manage her OCD. The organization provides referrals to therapists in your area who treat this form of anxiety. In July the foundation holds its annual conference with programs and workshops for people with OCD as well as their friends and loved ones. A special feature of the conference is the opportunity to have an individual half-hour meeting with an OCD expert.

BOOKS

Medication and Herbs

Herbs for the Mind by Jonathan Davidson, M.D., and Kathryn Conner, M.D. (Guilford Press)

Davidson and Conner are both psychiatrists at Duke University's Medical Center, where Davidson directs the Anxiety and Traumatic Stress Program. Both have extensively studied the effects of certain herbs on mood and emotions. This book gives concise, current information on how effective certain herbs are for the treatment of anxiety, stress, and depression. Of particular interest to *Soothe Your Nerves* readers are the chapters on kava kava and valerian.

The Pill Book edited by Harold M. Silverman (Bantam Books)

Updated every two years, this is an excellent layperson's guide to various medications and can be used when consulting your psychiatrist or family doctor about medication. It gives information about the brand and generic names of various medications, how the medication works in your body, and its benefits and side effects. *The Pill Book* is available in most drugstores as well as at the major bookstore chains.

Mental Health

Mental Health: Culture, Race, and Ethnicity (A Supplement to Mental Health: A Report of the Surgeon General)

Former Surgeon General David Satcher made mental health a top priority and wrote several major reports on the topic. This one is particularly helpful in understanding anxiety and depres-

sion in Black Americans. You can order it online at www.
surgeongeneral.gov or request a copy by writing to the Office
of the Surgeon General, 5600 Fishers Lane, Rockville, MD
20857.

Depression

Willow Weep for Me by Meri Nana-Ama Danquah (W.W. Norton & Company)

This is a beautifully written first-person account of a Black
woman living with depression. Her story has touched the lives
of thousands of Black women. A must-read for Black women
who are experiencing depression along with their anxiety difficulties.

Lay My Burden Down by Alvin F. Poussaint, M.D., and Amy
Alexander (Beacon Press)

Poussaint and Alexander, who both lost brothers to suicide,
provide an in-depth analysis of suicide and depression in the
African-American community. The authors give insight into
how life in America contributes to the development of depression in Black women and men.

Sister Circles

Sisters of the Yam: Black Women and Self-Recovery by bell
hooks (South End Press)

A great resource book for a Soothe Your Nerves Sister Circle or for any Strong Black Woman who would like to rest.
hooks reminds us of the importance of taking care of ourselves.

Sister Stepping Out with Attitude by Anita Richmond Bunkley (HarperPerennial)

A wonderful self-help book about letting go of the image of what others think you should be and pursuing your dreams, written especially for Black women. Yet another great resource for your Soothe Your Nerves Sister Circle.

In the Company of My Sisters by Julia Boyd (Dutton)

One of the first books written on Black women's mental health, Boyd uses the voices of the women in her sister circle to discuss Black women's self-esteem issues.

Menopause: The Mean-Pause by Clissie Rogers

Rogers's honesty about her hardheadedness, breakdown, and recovery is refreshing. This slim pamphlet is available by writing the author, Clissie Rogers, at 309 Dorchester Road, Akron, OH 44320. When you write, let her know you read about her pamphlet in *Soothe Your Nerves*.

Feel the Fear and Do It Anyway by Susan Jeffers, Ph.D. (Fawcett/Columbine)

Countless women of all races have benefited from the wisdom and exercises found in this book. This is a great book for everyone in your Soothe Your Nerves Sister Circle.

Healing for Damaged Emotions Workbook by David Seamands and Beth Funk (Chariot Victor)

I use this book in my Sunday morning sister circle class. If your Soothe Your Nerves Sister Circle is part of a Sunday school or church outreach program, this is a good book to combine with *Soothe Your Nerves*. The book is written from a Christian perspective. The women in the Sunday morning sister circle found the exercises and journaling particularly meaningful.

One Day at a Time in Phobics Victorious by Rosemary (Christopher Publishing House)

A Bible-based affirmation book for people suffering from specific and social phobias. Each daily affirmation begins with a Bible verse on anxiety and fear.

The Power of Positive Thinking by Dr. Norman Vincent Peale *(Prentice-Hall)*

A classic in the field, this book combines spiritual and psychological principles. Visualization and affirmation exercises abound. A booklet of spiritual affirmations compiled by Dr. Peale is available by writing to an address listed in the book.

Discrimination and Prejudice

A Foot in Each World by Leanita McClain (Northwestern University Press)

This collection of essays and columns is by the late columnist and first Black on the editorial board of the *Chicago Tribune*. Although all contributions were written in the early 1980s, the issues she discusses still ring true for Black women in the new millennium.

The Rage of the Privileged Class by Ellis Cose (HarperCollins)

This book addresses the anger experienced by middle-class Black men and women. Prejudice and discrimination can truly generate a great deal of stress.

Books to Affirm Your Spirit and Soothe Your Soul

Mama Day by Gloria Naylor (Vintage Contemporaries)

This novel features a woman with generalized anxiety. Mama Day's approach to alleviating that anxiety combines herbal remedies, motherwit, and cognitive behavioral techniques, and that's just the side story. The central story speaks to the power of family and love.

Zenzele: A Letter for My Daughter by J. Nozipo Maraire (Weidenfeld & Nicolson)

This novel is written in the form of a letter from a mother in Zimbabwe to her daughter, an Ivy League college student. With warmth, beauty, and humor this book addresses the question "What does it mean to be a Black woman?" This book will affirm the spirit of all in your Soothe Your Nerves Sister Circle.

Beloved by Toni Morrison (Alfred Knopf)

Several of my English professor friends say this is the best fiction book written about the impact of slavery on Black Americans. I believe they're right, but I also think that this book speaks to the healing power found in a community of Black women and of love. The secondary story of Sixo and the Thirty-Mile Woman is an added bonus.

Lanterns by Marian Wright Edelman (Beacon Press)

This book will remind you of who and what is important in life. A true lantern, someone who lights the way for you, is a precious gift.

The *Value in the Valley* and *Yesterday, I Cried* by Iyanla Vanzant (Simon & Schuster)

The first book will remind you that in the midst of a storm there is hope and a valuable life lesson to learn. The second book will help you forgive yourself. Both will affirm your spirit and soothe your soul.

Tar Beach by Faith Ringold (Crown Publishers)
When you walk into my office, this is the first book you see. *Tar Beach* is a story that teaches you and your children how to fly.

WEBSITES

Rise Sally Rise®, Inc.
www.risesallyrise.com
330-630-5792
E-mail: risesallyrise@yahoo.com

My website. Rise Sally Rise® features information and tools to help women overcome anxiety and fear from a psychological, spiritual, and Black perspective. Be sure to check out our monthly serial, *Bad Nerves,* and the resource page for Soothe Your Nerves Sister Circles.

Something Within: A Quarterly Newsletter
www.somethingwithin.com
P.O. Box 281734
Nashville, TN 37228
Fax: 615-299-0583
E-mail: sowithin@bellsouth.net

This electronic newsletter published by author, minister, and divinity school professor Renita J. Weems is for women seeking balance and wholeness. The articles, pictures, and reviews are written to help Black women deal with the discrimination and stressors in their lives.

BIBLIOGRAPHY

Barlow, D. H. (2002). *Anxiety and Its Disorders: The Nature and Treatment of Anxiety and Panic* (2nd ed.). New York: Guilford.

Canfield, J., and Hansen, M. V. (1995). *The Aladdin Factor*. New York: Berkley.

Conner, K. M., and Vaughan, D. S. (1999). *Kava: Nature's Stress Relief*. New York: Avon Books.

Cose, E. (1993). *The Rage of a Privileged Class*. New York: HarperCollins.

Craske, M. G.; Barlow, D. H.; and O'Leary, T. A. (1992). *Mastery of Your Anxiety and Worry: Therapist's Guide*. Albany, NY: Graywind.

Craske, M. G.; Meadows, E.; and Barlow, D. H. (1994). *Therapist's Guide for Mastery of Your Anxiety and Panic II*. Albany, NY: Graywind.

Davidson, J. T., and Conner, K. (2000). *Herbs for the Mind*. New York: Guilford.

Dossey, L. (1993). *Healing Words*. San Francisco: HarperSanFrancisco.

Fowler, J. (1981). *Stages of Faith: The Psychology of Human Development and the Quest for Meaning*. San Francisco: HarperSanFrancisco.

Franklin, A., and Ritz, D. (1999). *Aretha: From These Roots*. New York: Villard.

Friedman, S.; Paradis, C. M.; and Hatch, M. (1994). "Characteristics of African-American and White Patients with Panic Disorder and Agoraphobia." *Hospital and Community Psychiatry* 45(8): 798–803.

———. (1994). "Issues of Misdiagnosis in Panic Disorder with Agoraphobia." In S. Friedman (ed.), *Anxiety Disorders in African-Americans*. New York: Springer.

Garber, S. W.; Garber, M. D.; and Spizman, M. D. (1993). *Monsters Under the Bed*. New York: Villard.

Gayles, G. W. (1991). *Anointed to Fly*. New York: Harlem River Press.

Gravitz, H. (1998). *Obsessive Compulsive Disorder: New Help for the Family*. Santa Barbara, CA: Healing Visions Press.

Greenberg, P. E., et al. "The Economic Burden of Anxiety Disorders in the 1990s." *Journal of Clinical Psychiatry* 60(7): 427–35.

hooks, b. (1993). *Sisters of the Yam: Black Women and Self-Recovery*. Boston: South End Press.

Hull, G. T.; Bell-Scott, P.; and Smith, B. *But Some of Us Brave*. New York: Feminist Press.

Jeffers, S. (1987). *Feel the Fear and Do It Anyway*. New York: Fawcett Columbine.

Lee, M. D. (director) (2000). *The Best Man*. Videocassette. Universal City, CA: Universal Studios.

Lorde, A. (1980). *The Cancer Journals*. Argyle, NY: Spinsters.

Markway, B. G., and Markway, G. P. (2001). *Painfully Shy*. New York: St. Martin's.

McHenry, D. (director) (2001). *Kingdom Come*. Videocassette. Beverly Hills, CA: Twentieth-Century-Fox Home Entertainment.

Neal, A. M.; Nagle Rich, L.; and Smucker, W. D. (1994). "The Presence of Panic Disorder Among African-American Hypertensives." *Journal of Black Psychology* 20: 29–35.

Neal, A. M., and Turner, S. M. (1991). "Anxiety Disorders Research and African Americans: Current Status." *Psychological Bulletin* 109: 400–10.

Neal, A. M., and Wilson, M. (1989). "The Role of Skin Color and Facial Features in the Black Community: Implications for Black Women and Therapy." *Clinical Psychology Review* 9: 323–33.

Neal-Barnett, A. M. (2001). "Being Black: New Thoughts on the Old Phenomenon of Acting White." In A. M. Neal-Barnett, J. Contreras, and K. Kerns (eds.), *Forging Links: African-American Children Clinical Developmental Perspectives*. Westport, CT: Praeger.

Neal-Barnett, A. M. (1999). OCD: Multi-Cultural Issues. Available at www.ocfoundation.org.

Neal-Barnett, A. M., and Crowther, J. (2000). "To Be Female, Anxious, Middle-Class, and Black." *Psychology of Women Quarterly* 24(2): 132–40.

Neal-Barnett, A. M., and Smith, J. M. Sr. (1997). "Assessment and Treatment of Anxious African Americans." In S. Friedman (ed.), *Treating Anxiety Across Cultures*. New York: Guilford, pp. 154–74.

————. (1996). "Behavior Therapy and African-American Children: Considering an Afrocentric Approach." *Cognitive Behavior and Practice* 3: 351–69.

Poussaint, A. F., and Alexander, A. (2000). *Lay My Burden Down*. Boston: Beacon Press.

Rapoport, J. L. (1989). *The Boy Who Couldn't Stop Washing*. New York: Dutton.

Reibel, D. K., et al. (2001). "Mindfulness-based Stress Reduction and Health-Related Quality of Life in a Heterogeneous Patient Population." *General Hospital Psychiatry* 23: 183–92.

Robbins-Brinson, L. M., and Neal-Barnett, A. M. (February 1997). "Defending My Research or Defending My Ethnicity." *The Behavior Therapist* 20(2): 17–19.

Sampson, S. (2001). "Being Female and Anxious." *ADAA Reporter* 12(3): 1, 8–9

Schwartz, J. (1996). *Brain Lock*. New York: ReganBooks.

Seamands, D., and Funk, B. (1992). *Healing for Damaged Emotions Workbook*. Colorado Springs: Chariot Victor Publishing.

Taylor, S., et al. (2000). "Biobehavioral Responses to Stress in Females: Tend-and-Befriend, not Fight-or-Flight." *Psychological Review* 107(3): 411–29.

U.S. Department of Health and Human Services (2001). *Mental Health: Culture, Race, and Ethnicity. A Supplement to Mental Health: A Report of the Surgeon General*. Rockville, MD: U.S. Department of Health and Human Services, Substance Abuse and Mental Health Services Administration, Center for Mental Health Services.

Walker, M. A., and Singleton, K. B. (1999). *Natural Health for African Americans*. New York: Warner Books.

Wallace, M. (1980). *Black Macho and the Myth of Superwoman*. New York: Warner Books.

Weinstock, L. (1998). *Overcoming Panic Disorder: A Woman's Guide*. Lincolnwood, IL: Contemporary Books.

Williams, K. P. (1993). *How to Help Your Loved One Recover from Agoraphobia*. Far Hills, NJ: New Horizon Press.

Williams, K. E.; Chambless, D. L.; and Steketee, G. (1998). "Behavioral Treatment of Obsessive-Compulsive Disorder in African Americans: Clinical Issues." *Journal of Behavior Therapy and Experimental Psychiatry* 23(6): 161–70.

ACKNOWLEDGMENTS

I have always wondered why the acknowledgments section of any book is so long. After writing one, I know why. This book would not exist except for the encouragement and support of nine women, one teenager, one husband, two agents, one editor, two libraries, one sister circle, and one little girl.

From the inception of this book I've been blessed with the counsel of nine spiritual women:

Gloria McCullough, who coached this book into existence;
Dr. Sharon Bell, who prayed it into being and held my hand while I was writing it;
Carla Davis, who sang, critiqued, and advised me to watch my tenses from the very first draft to the final version;
Doris L. Neal, my mother, who with her band of prayer warriors prayed over every word I wrote;
Betsey Neal Robinson, my big sister, who provided me with unrestrained enthusiasm;
Linda Neal Moore, my little sister, who provided me with the voice of reason;

Trisha Neal, my sister-in-law, who not only encouraged me but made sure I looked good while writing, speaking, or teaching about the topic;
Dr. Linda Walker, who so willingly shared with me her vast knowledge of gospel music; and
Dr. Gail Elizabeth Wyatt, my other "big sister," who reminded me I had a story to tell in the first place.

The energy of one teenager:
Talia Robinson spent the bulk of her summer and fall talking, laughing, swimming, reading, drawing, painting nails, and doing somersaults with my daughter. Special thanks to Talia's parents for allowing her to work for us.

Tremendous growth and change:
From the women in my Sunday morning sister circle class. Ladies, your willingness to open your hearts and minds had a profound impact on this book.

The support of a wonderful spouse:
Edgar J. Barnett Jr. built my office, went to gymnastics, sang in Kindermusik, shopped for groceries, and sold at least one hundred advance copies of the book while I was writing it.

The unbridled truth from my agents:
This book is better because of the input of Madeleine Morel and Barbara Lowenstein.

Creative suggestions from my editor:
Cherise Grant.

Great research skills and patience from two libraries:
Paul Fehrman and the team of research librarians at Kent
State University found the answer to every question I asked
and some I didn't. Truly, if you want to know something,
ask a librarian. The staff of the Wooster and Tallmadge
branches of the Akron Summit County Public Library
System made only one comment about the overdue books:
"We know you are eventually going to return them, Dr.
Barnett."

Unconditional love from "the diva":
My daughter, Reece, changed CDs, drew pictures, gave me
big hugs and kisses, pushed the print button, helped record
the answering machine message, and wrote her own book,
Gammaw and Pop-Pop by Dr. Reece Barnett, while I was
writing this one.

INDEX

❖

ABOUT THE AUTHOR

Dr. Angela Neal-Barnett is an award-winning psychologist and nationally recognized expert on anxiety disorders among African Americans. She has authored numerous articles and book chapters on the topic, and her research is cited in the Surgeon General's report, *Mental Health: Culture, Race, and Ethnicity*. Dr. Barnett directs the Program for Research on Anxiety Disorders among African Americans and is the recipient of grants from the National Institute of Mental Health, National Institutes of Health, Ohio Children's Trust Fund, Ohio Commission on Minority Health, Ohio Board of Regents, and the Health Priorities Trust Fund.

A recipient of the American Psychological Association's Kenneth and Mamie Clark Award for Outstanding Contribution to the Professional Development of Ethnic Minority Graduate Students, Dr. Barnett also served on the faculty of the Harvard-NIH-Kellogg–funded Next Generation Project. She directs the Kent State University psychology group, a program designed to give undergraduates of color the knowledge, skills, and attitude to succeed in graduate school.

A sought-after workshop presenter, Dr. Barnett has been a speaker at national conferences, endowed lecture series, panel discussions, and professional group assemblies around the country. Her work has been featured in national magazines and on national television, including CNN and BET. A member of the psychology faculty at Kent State University, she is also the CEO and founder of Rise Sally Rise®, Inc., a business dedicated to helping women and children overcome anxiety and fear via programs that incorporate a psychological, spiritual, and Black perspective.

Dr. Neal-Barnett received her B.A. from Mount Union College (Alliance, Ohio) and her M.A. and Ph.D. from DePaul University (Chicago). She also completed a renowned postdoctoral fellowship in anxiety disorders at the University of Pittsburgh School of Medicine's Western Psychiatric Institute and Clinic. Neal-Barnett is listed in *Who's Who in America, Who's Who in the Midwest, Who's Who in American Women, Who's Who in Medicine and Health Care, Who's Who Among African Americans, Who's Who in Business and Industry,* and *Outstanding Americans. Northern Ohio Live* magazine has named her one of the five hundred most influential women in northeastern Ohio.

Printed in the United States
By Bookmasters